What they are saying about
"Romancing The Voters"

Review by: Tony Krvaric : ☆ ☆ ☆ ☆ ☆

Fred Schnaubelt has done a lot of research, compiling interesting, entertaining, and insightful arguments for Liberty-minded Americans who are constantly under fire from "progressive" elites. This handy compendium of political issues is something that can easily be reviewed before engaging in a discussion. Great for "Teachable Moments."

-Tony Krvaric, Chairman, Republican Party of San Diego County

Review by: Lawrence Reed : ☆ ☆ ☆ ☆ ☆

At a time when common sense seems endangered, along comes Fred Schnaubelt with a book of useful information and rhetorical devices that put common sense back into political debate. If you want to influence others for good or just put the bad guys in their place, get this book and keep it handy.

-Lawrence W. Reed, President, Foundation for Economic Education (www.fee.org)

Review by: Mike McFee : ☆ ☆ ☆ ☆

What an excellent compilation and insightful prose on the current direction of American Politics. Mr. Schnaubelt hit this one out of the park. Truly a great historically relevant guidebook, which should be required reading for EVERY congressman today. As an elected official, I appreciate the elevation of these important issues and the historical basis for his writing. Well done!

-Michael McFee, City Council, Beaufort, SC

Review by: Jim Elliott : ☆ ☆ ☆ ☆ ☆

Fred Schnaubelt's book should be read by all concerned citizens. I have created millions of political direct mail pieces for candidates of both parties. We need sensible elected officials. Support your candidate...write a check or walk precincts. Better yet run for office. America needs you.

-Jim Elliott, President, Western Graphics, Lemon Grove CA

Review by: Lynette Williams: ★ ★ ★ ★ ★

You who read this book already know many of your liberal leaning friends have become oblivious to the outside world because they are preoccupied with their favorite things. They need to be persuaded how to think for themselves, with these new approaches, instead of being indoctrinated by the main stream media. You can be the one who exposes them to economic fallacies and facts that will help turn around their point of view. Romancing the Voters will give you the skills necessary to peg misinformed people the instant you begin a conversation with them.

Read this book with a pencil in hand. Label sentences that stand out on how to respond to a fallacy, hypocrisy, truth, historical fact, common sense, opinion, horrid or whatever label seems right to you. Write a summary of the most meaningful parts of each chapter.

The SECOND time you read the book, develop a color system to highlight statements, such as orange for truths, yellow for exposing fallacies, blue for key facts (such as the last sentence on page 79), green for hypocrisies. Romancing the Voters is going to become one of the most dog-eared books in your library.

The knowledge you gain from this brief handbook will change the way you converse about politics. You will make your case more appealing as you develop Ronald Reagan style anecdotes (page 87). You will learn to redefine words liberals use, such as changing 'minimum wage' to 'learning wage' (page 55). Best of all, you can stop being silent when confronted with issues you are hesitant to defend because you don't want to make a fool of yourself. With this arsenal of talking points you won't be at a loss for words anymore!

-Lynette Gain Williams, President, Women Volunteers in Politics, San Diego, CA

Review by: Colin Flaherty : ★ ★ ★ ★ ★

There are two things you should do with this book: 1) Read it. You will learn something important and something funny. I guarantee it. I got a kick out of this quote: ""If you don't read the newspaper, you're uninformed. If you read the newspaper, you're misinformed." Mark Twain. And 2) Give it as a gift. Even low information voters will get a kick out the in trenches observations that have made Fred Schnaubelt one of the most interesting and distinguished observers and political actors in San Diego. Ever. So get it.

-Colin Flaherty, author, *White Girl Bleed A Lot*

Review by: Richard Wira : ★ ★ ★ ★ ★

Romancing the Voters, don't get Honeyfuggled is a great handbook for Toastmasters with ideas for at least 15 tested talks. Every week Toastmasters are confronted with, 'What should I talk about?' This book will stimulate your thought process regarding many of the questions we are facing today. It will give you ample material to draw from and form your own conclusions. It's a great read because all of the information is out there; we just don't have the time to look it up for ourselves."

-Richard Wira, Toastmasters International World Champions of Public Speaking, 2006 Finalist

Review by: Eric Andersen : ★ ★ ★ ★ ★

Former San Diego City Councilman Fred Schnaubelt continues to make himself invaluable to the common man. Romancing the Voters is designed to equip and protect us from the false ideas we face regularly from our local politicians. I look forward each month to receiving Fred's thoughtful economic insights and analysis and value having a more comprehensive compilation of his ideas.

-Eric Andersen, co-founder im2moro (www.im2moro.com)

Review by: Darrell Beck : ⭐⭐⭐⭐⭐

Every Tea Party member should have a copy of "Romancing the Voters" written by Fred Schnaubelt as reference to historic facts and to avoid being "honeyfuggled" within the world of extreme political chicanery. It answers many questions posed by "progressives" to humiliate and demean patriots who are merely trying to restore our constitutional republic. **-Darrell Beck, Ramona Tea'd, member steering committee**

Review by: David Bogan : ⭐⭐⭐⭐⭐

Thought provoking, rational discussion points defending the views of the "rest of us" who prefer to think on our own and not regurgitate the slanted interpretation in the mainstream media. He points out the morsels of history conveniently forgotten or buried by today's pundits. Fred intelligently teaches us to look at the actions, not just listen to the words of politicians to understand their true beliefs. He gives us a pleasant, informative guide to navigate the slippery landscapes that are today's headlines.

-David Bogan

Review by: Brian Brady: ⭐⭐⭐⭐⭐

Fred Schnaubelt cuts through the BS and explains the silly side of politics (campaigning) while revealing how dangerous the serious side of politics (governing) is today. He reveals how politicians have figured out how to play "Santa Claus" and "buy" votes by making ridiculous promises. God help us because some of them actually keep those ridiculous promises. A champion of the limited government movement, Fred offers a centuries old remedy for that which ails us---constitutionally constrained government. This is an easy read. It's entertaining, each topic is relatively short, and Fred's writing style is easy to understand. Buy this book.

-Brian Brady

Review by: Priscilla Schreiber: ⭐⭐⭐⭐⭐

Fred Schnaubelt, has written a gem of a handbook for those of us who consider ourselves liberty-minded "freedom riders". His exhaustive research and personal experience in politics gives us a renewed understanding in the art of using political talking points. "Romancing the Voter..." is an engaging twist for disarming our friends who may think differently. Fred's book is a well chronicled mixture of historical facts and commentaries for such a time as this. **- Priscilla Schreiber**

Review by: Jim Elliott : ⭐⭐⭐⭐⭐

Fred Schnaubelt's book should be read by all concerned citizens. I have created millions of political direct mail pieces for candidates of both parties. We need sensible elected officials. Support your candidate...write a check or walk precincts. Better yet run for office. America needs you.

-Jim Elliott, President, Western Graphics, Lemon Grove CA

Review by: Monte: ⭐⭐⭐⭐⭐

I'm a proud owner of "Romancing the Voter's" and am learning a lot about a lot of things by reading it. I was really impressed to learn that you had a conversation with Ronald Reagan and brought Walter Williams and Thomas Sowell to a city council meeting. Good Job Fred and Thank You.

-Monte

Review by: Art Schmitz: ⭐⭐⭐⭐⭐

This is a great book and should be required reading by every high school student before graduating. It's simple enough that even elementary school students would be able to enjoy it.

-Art Schmitz, Citizens For Private Property Rights

Romancing The Voters
(Political Talking Points)

By Fred Schnaubelt

Test Your Political IQ

Are you embarrassed when your friends know these answers and you don't?
Now you can know more than your associates, reporters and politicians.

(Compare your knowledge before and after reading this book)

Do You Know?

" Who said, "I've been rich and I've been poor, and rich is better"
" No President since 1904 has received a majority vote from the VEP?
" When Bill Gates <u>walks</u> into McDonalds, statistically everyone's a billionaire?
" President Obama won the Presidency with 31% of VEP (Registered Voters)?
" Local elected officials can win a Primary Election with fewer than 5% of VEP?
" Government is not a necessary evil, but indispensable for a free market?
" Why liberals and conservatives think differently?
" Who said, "The U.S. has the richest poor people in the world"?
" That the founders intentionally established a system of perpetual Gridlock?
" Newspapers don't print the truth, they print what people say?
" Why President Obama's health care bill is 2,700 pages long?
" Liberals, on average, contribute 30% less than conservatives to charities?
" Do you know that government employees do not pay any income taxes?
" Why most businessmen (big business) are not defenders of free enterprise?
" Waste and Fraud will never go away?
" You're 11-times more likely to be <u>shot</u> by a policeman than an armed citizen?
" If you earned $113,799 in 2009, the IRS put you in the top 10%?
" That 86% of Fortune 500 companies in 1959 were gone from the list by 2009?
" 89 countries have higher murder rates than the U.S.?
" Reports of "children" killed by guns are due to juvenile gang members?
" Police fired 200 rounds to kill just one of the two Boston Marathon Bombers?
" Secret Service Agents change 10 round clips of ammunition in one second?
" Who thinks it is "unfair" for smart, talented people to succeed?
" Gasoline a gallon "adjusted for inflation" (2012) was 29 cents less than in 1918?
" Europe has had as many mass killings as the U.S.?
" Who said, "I want to move to a country where the poor people are fat"?
" Why the so-called "Public Good" is impossible to determine?
" "If you don't read the newspaper, you're uninformed, if you do mis-informed"?
" The Ku Klux Klan was indicted as a "terrorist" arm of the Democratic Party?
" Scotland Yard reported 6 times as many murders by knives as by guns?
" Children are 14 times killed more by cars and bicycles than by guns?
" Less than 1% of criminals get their guns at "Gun Shows"?
" Why TEA PARTY members are so hated and vilified?
" What Barack Obama, Ronald Reagan, Bill Clinton, Sarah Palin share?
" How to prove Liberalism has been a colossal failure?
" Taxpayers don't "ask" for government services with less taxes and who does?
" States with greatest increases in guns have the largest drops in crime?
" Why "Society" is at fault for crime frequently cited is a stupid statement?
" What country sentenced a killer to 3.3 months in prison for each child he killed?
" Why everyone in Zimbabwe is a billionaire?
" The minimum wage in reality is a "learning Wage"?
" Foreigners trained in America cannot make as much in their own country?
" The Death Penalty is an absolute deterrent to murder?
" Very few people receiving the minimum wage use it to support families?
" Why America is Rich?
" The only way to increases the "general" standard of living in any country?
" The top 3% of income tax filers pay more than the other 97%?
" Why the government's Bread and Circuses ended in ancient Rome?

8

" That 10,000 "Baby Boomers" retire each day with a life expectancy of 85 years?
" The average American worker has saved less than $25,000 for retirement?
" Some politicians think taxing less than 100% of your income is a " Loophole"?
" One result of raising the "learning wage" (minimum wage) – is idle teenagers?
" That 96% of members of Congress give the other 4% a bad name?
" Less than 5% of the workforce is paid the minimum wage?
" That there are six measures of unemployment, U-1 to U-6, and why U-3 is used?
" Why so many countries are poor?
" What is the single most important resource for creating wealth?
" The "Public Good," or "Good of the Community," are fictions of the mind?
" 94% of millionaires are no longer millionaires after 9 years?
" Why tax cuts for the rich don't give the rich anything?
" Why quintiles of rich and poor don't represent the rich and poor as individuals?
" Why it is easier for the poor to become rich than rich people to become richer?
" That minimum wage increases often result in increases in crime?
" Why the Democrat Party has been the "party of the rich" for decades?
" That 7 of the 10 richest members of Congress are Democrats?
" Republican claims of reducing spending historically have been a farce?
" Counting $1 dollar a second takes 2,000 years to count cost of Social Security?
" Why so many "good" people depend on government for cradle to grave care?
" Why Social Security obligations are not paid in a lump sum upon retirement?
" Why American has the "richest" poor people in the world?
" Why the poor of the world are becoming richer than ever in history?
" Why your neighbors working for government are unqualified to make decisions?
" How much was collected when it was said, Taxes are cost of a civilized society?
" Less than 1% of all wage earners receive minimum wage after 3 years?
"The cliché, "The rich get richer and the poor get poorer" is pure Buffalo Chips?
" With a half million dollars you can still be called poor by the government?
" The sun is finite but inexhaustible?
" Why the supply of oil, while finite, is inexhaustible?
" Who are the primary beneficiaries of increases in the minimum wage?
" Federal government spending has shrunk only four times in 62 years?
 " Prior to 1948 minimum wage increases Blacks had lower unemployment rates?
" When Social Security was initiated, the life expectancy was 65 years?
" There are three kinds of lies: lies, damned lies, and statistics?
" It took until 1800 for the world population to reach one billion people?
" This year it is estimated world population will reach 7 billion?
" Over 10-years half the poor people (bottom quintile) move to higher quintiles?
" Over 10-years half the rich people (top quintile) move into a lower quintile?
" How oil speculation benefits you and society as a whole?
" The Census reports of 15% living in poverty, nearly 3/4 own a car, 1/3 own two?
" The top 20% of families have twice as many people working as bottom 20%?
" Your gas costs less per pound than cost of delivering mail across the street?
" The U.S. is purported to hold more gas and oil than all of Saudi Arabia?
" That government derives its income from force, coercion or violence?
" In 2009 nearly 26 million non-paying income tax filers received over $57 billion?
" Why getting the right people in government is not the problem?
" A gallon of gasoline costs less today than two 1964 dimes?
" Martin Luther King was a Republican and Why?
" The ideal tax gets the most feathers out of the goose with the least squawk?
" How the rules determine the outcome of the game?
   Hint: In basketball make everyone play in high heels.

(Compare your knowledge before and after reading this book)

9

Special thanks

Kevin Schnaubelt, Technical Coordinator

Catherine Jaime, Editor

Homeschool Author and Speaker

Books at http://www.CatherineJaime.com

E-books at
https://www.smashwords.com/profile/view/CatherineJaime

Paperbacks at https://www.amazon.com/author/catherinejaime

Homeschool information at
http://www.CreativeLearningConnection.com

Library of Congress LCCN # 2013911214

You can also order the Online e-book Romancing the Voters for gifts from Smashwords ISBN: 9781301186259 : Epub (Apple iPad/iBooks, Nook, Sony Reader, Kobo, and most e-reading apps including Stanza, Aldiko, Adobe Digital Editions) LRF (Use only for older model Sony Readers that don't support .epub)
https://www.smashwords.com/books/view/302807

Romancing The Voters Kindle ASIN: B00E152L8E

Watch Fred's TV interview@https://www.RomancingTheVoters.com

ISBN-13: 978-1490317823

ISBN-10: 1490317821

Copyright 2013

Edition, July 4, 2013

FOREWORD

You can depend on this brief handbook when you need to be quickly conversant on issues you do not have time to research. Political Cross Dressing is the art of using your adversary's own talking points against him or her. It is vitally important to learn both sides of various issues to avoid being blind-sided. We all hold contradictory beliefs; we understand the meaning of words differently. You can use this to your advantage. Politics and elections today are about who gets nearly $4 trillion of government spending (2013) and who pays for it. This Handbook is a compilation of some of the most persuasive responses to numerous political issues, taken from over 500 books. Those issues that resurface year after year in the press and in friendly discussions. The best part: You do not have to buy all 500 books to get the most cogent nuggets.

ACKNOWLEDGMENTS

I am indebted to the following whose writings/teachings have contributed mightily to the political issues addressed in an easy to read Handbook. This thin, concise book is designed to give you more than a "Bumper Sticker" response to some of the major issues of the day, and test the things you know, or think you know, or believe are right, and determine if your learning has been superficial.

My Thanks To:

Adam Smith, Leonard Read, Ben Rogge and the faculty of the Foundation for Economic Education, Dale Carnegie, The Reason Foundation, The Cato Institute, American Enterprise Institute, Barry Goldwater, Henry Hazlitt, Ludwig von Mises, Ayn Rand, Milton Friedman, Friedrich Hayek, James Buchanan, Henry George, John Kenneth Galbraith, John Rawls, Charles Reich, Murray Rothbard, Fyodor Dostoevsky, Wayne Perryman, Walter Williams, Thomas Sowell, and my friend, mentor, and Best Man, Professor, Bernie Siegan.

Any misinterpretation of their teachings is my fault and mine alone.

Table of Contents

Chapter 6   48

Why Is America Rich?

Americans are richer today in most ways than were kings and queens, princes and potentates historically.

Chapter 7   53

Media Ignore Individuals in Gap between Rich and Poor

When billionaire Bill Gates walks into McDonald's, the "average income" of all skyrockets to more than $1 billion.

Chapter 8   57

Increasing Minimum Wage Would Generate Adverse Result

Those calling for raising the "learning wage" to $9.00 declare even this is not enough to live on, why the hypocrisy? Why not $22.00 an hour?

Chapter 9   61

The 47 percent Who Don't Pay Taxes

The Democratic Party has been the "party of the rich" for decades, led by rich media manipulators.

Chapter 10   65

The Gap Between Ignorance, Misinformation, Disinformation

"A cause of many of our mistakes and problems is ignorance — ignorance of the facts about the rest of the world.

Chapter 1

Democracy and Majority Vote Not What You Think

"Under our Constitution it is We The People who are sovereign. The people have the final say. The legislators are their spokesmen. The people determine through their votes the destiny of the nation."
---Justice William O. Douglas

Contrary to what Justice Douglas said, the people do not determine through their votes, the destiny of the nation, at least not through a democracy by so-called majority vote. "Democracy," simply means majority rule --- for good or bad. The heart of politics is the art of romancing the voters (pretending with intent to deceive).

No U.S. President or Congress has ever represented the majority of the people, and in fact, almost never more than a third of the Voter Eligible Population (VEP). Once elected, however, most politicians believe that a first kiss inexorably leads to a total surrender of virtue and thereafter think they can honeyfuggle the voters whenever --- and on whatever issue --- they choose.

Facts are stubborn things. Americans, in reality, are ruled by factions. If the media reported the facts about how few votes win elections, Presidents and for that matter, all elected officials would never have the chutzpah to do what they do. Politicians would have to return to being administrative watchdogs over the public purse, as originally intended.

Since Teddy Roosevelt (1904), no President has received more than 36% support from the voter-eligible-population (VEP). A country divided is not something new, or something old.

President Obama won just 31% of the VEP. The media characterizes this plurality of votes as a mandate to justify the President (any President for that matter) imposing his will, or vision upon us. Not one President in over 100 years, in fact, has received a legitimate mandate to impose his vision on America.

15

This also applies to nearly all elected officials who rarely receive more than 27%, some less than 10% of the VEP. As Casey Stengel used to say, "You can look it up!" Check with your Registrar of Voters.

"Newspapers don't print the truth they print what people say."
                                                    Rick Paddock, L.A. Times

It's important to understand this reality. It explains a lot. Think about it. Reporters covering politics seek out a catchy quote --- or they make up a controversial one --- and ask for a response. Then they print what is said. Reporters vie for as many readers' "attention" as possible. That is what headlines are about (and teaser TV spots). You have to get someone's attention before they can become interested in what you write.

The rules of the game determine the outcome of any contest. For instance, most people agree no woman's basketball team can beat the L.A. Lakers. But change just one rule and you'll get a different outcome: make everyone play in high heels. The rules of politics (for those actually turning out to vote) are the ancient doctrine of "might makes right" whereby 50% plus one = 100% and 50% minus one = 0. This boils down to "We won --- Elections have consequences --- Get over it."

Fortunately, we do not live in a Democracy. When Benjamin Franklin departed from the Constitutional Convention of 1787, he was asked, what kind of government did you give us? Franklin replied, "A 'Republic' if you can keep it."

In fact, the founders loathed democracy. They knew democracies often descended into Mobocracies (today, think Libya and Egypt), and did everything they could to guard against "Majoritarianism." They tried to developed a vaccine (a republic) against the contagion of "popular delusions and the madness of crowds" so politics would not be infected. They knew that Plato and Aristotle thought democracy ultimately led to tyranny.

They created a system whereby Senators are elected for six years, Presidents four years and Congressmen two years so the entire elected body could never be swept up in the passions of a movement. One Senator represents about 19 million people in California but only 288,000 in Wyoming, which makes it hard to contend that voting is equal representation or majority vote.

The founders gave the several small states, regardless of population, equal representation in the Senate as an incentive to join the Union. To make doubly sure the populace could not be swept up by unforeseen events they created the Electoral College to trump the popular will. They believed it would not be possible to bribe all the electors of all the states at the same time.

For good measure, the founders established an unelected Supreme Court, whose members do not have to worry about running for office, which can overrule any majority vote.

The entire system they designed acts as a buffer against a popular, charming, captivating, charismatic orator (aka, A Cult of Personality).

PRAY FOR GRIDLOCK

Hard as they tried they never imagined a time where all of the problems attributed to an unaccountable federal government would be the result of compromises between factions (later called Democrats and Republicans) and a compliant press.

Compromises, however, are how we got a $16 trillion national debt. We should pray for gridlock. What we call "gridlock" the founders called "checks and balances." They fully intended to pit ambition against ambition. Whenever there is gridlock it is a win, win for the taxpayers.

The media, bless their hearts, keeps reporting that the American public demands things for which it is unwilling to be taxed. It's not the silent majority surprisingly, that is asking for endless handouts.

Most Congressional spending as reported in a 1991 study by James Payne confirmed that of 1,400 witnesses before Congress only seven could clearly be classified as opposed to spending.

More significant however, *"Of 1060 Congressional witnesses in favor of spending, 47 percent were federal administrators, and another 10 percent were state and local officials. An additional 6 percent were congressmen themselves."* In other words, 63 percent of the pro-spending witnesses were from government.

There is little doubt a similar ratio of supplicants demanding other people's money occurs before local city councils, supervisors, and state legislatures.

Very few responsible people "expect" something for nothing from government, although politicians are diligently trying to change this in exchange for votes.

Proposition 13 in California was one of those rare events which proved politicians can say "no, no, no" to the "gimme, gimme, gimme" crowd and still get elected. I know, I supported 13 and got elected.

"ALL POLITICAL POWER DERIVES FROM WHAT YOU CAN DO TO --- OR --- FOR SOMEONE"

Whenever you think the government is doing something stupid --- follow the money. If you want to understand politics assume 100% of what a politician says and does is for votes and campaign contributions.

A cardinal rule of politics is "watch what they do, not what they say." The actions of the few straight arrows are too rare to matter.

There is an old joke that 96% of the members of Congress give the other 4% a bad name.

People attracted to political office seem to have been born with two extra genes – the tax gene and the regulatory gene. They want to tax everything that moves or stands still and even tax the very air we breathe through a carbon footprint tax.

Can you think of any significant business they don't want to tax or regulate?

18

The story goes that Senator Edward Kennedy was listening to a speaker who began, *"Let me tax your memories for a moment"* whereupon Kennedy immediately exclaimed, *"Why didn't I think of that."*

"DEMOCRACY IS THE THEORY THAT THE COMMON PEOPLE KNOW WHAT THEY WANT, AND DESERVE TO GET IT GOOD AND HARD."
                                                                        -- H.L. Mencken

Consider the brilliant, beguiling, billionaire Mayor of New York, Michael Bloomberg who wants to regulate not only 16-ounce sodas, but also salt, butter, trans fats, popcorn, milkshakes, guns, and prohibit tobacco products from being displayed in public.

Other politicians want to tell us how to flush our toilets, what light bulbs to use, regulate guns, and health care, prohibit us from spanking our children, decree no smoking in our own homes, regulate potato chips, car colors (California 2009), etc., etc., etc., all for our own good. Both political parties have succeeded in turning free market Capitalism into overbearing "Regulated Capitalism."

Do not misunderstand; government is not a necessary evil, as often heard. It is absolutely necessary for a free society to work, but it should act as an umpire in enforcing the rules and should not be playing the game using its monopoly on force and violence. We cannot afford to have politicians continuously discrediting the government by their actions. Only when government is limited to its proper role can it earn and retain our respect.

The latest clever device used by government is to hide behind the cloak of complexity by passing laws with thousands of pages. *"We have to pass it to know what's in it,"* was House Speaker, Nancy Pelosi's response to the 2,700-page Obamacare Bill (with 20,000 pages of implementing rules).

James Madison in Federalist Paper 37 warned us against *"the obscurity arising from complexity."*

Since many laws today, particularly in the tax code and health care are incomprehensible --- who gets absolute power under their obscurity?

The answer is whoever has the power to interpret them. Without transparency, it is the politicians, planners and poseurs who interpret them on a daily basis.

We are told, "Ignorance of the law is no defense," implying we are supposed to know all 200,000 pages of laws on the books that were identified in a 2006 review.

The founders were aware of politics in practice for 180 years from the founding of Jamestown in 1607 to 1787. They were not neophytes and had learned from the experience of others about governing.

They understood that majority vote might be appropriate for selecting politicians to administer laws, but wholly inappropriate for voting on which laws to implement. This is why they gave us a republic with representatives chosen to make informed decisions.

Even so, on various issues, both Republicans and Democrats have changed sides over the years as easily as changing a suit of clothes.

Before becoming President, then Senator Obama railed against President Bush's budget deficits. Seems pretty funny now. Recently Democrat Congressman John Conyers said, *"Deficits don't matter."* Under President George W. Bush, it was Republican Dick Cheney saying, *"Deficits don't matter."*

Republican President, Dwight Eisenhower, however, said, *"...there must be balanced budgets."* Sometimes the party in power favors "Free Trade," sometimes not, favors the Patriot Act, sometimes not, or favors closing Gitmo, sometimes not.

When you get to taxes, Liberals argue that raising taxes will increase needed revenues to the government while Conservatives argue that lowering taxes will increase needed revenues to the government. Beyond the core functions of government --- we should ask: revenues needed for what?

Who knows best how to get the greatest benefits for the greatest number of people from "investing" money --- the government --- or those who know how to earn it --- a Bill Gates or a Joe Biden?

After the Presidency, real power in Washington resides in the Congressional committee chairmen as evidenced by the amount of campaign money they raise. Why do you think there are over 12,000 lobbyists in Washington D.C. spending a "reported" $3.3 billion annually?

If all political power comes from what you can do to --- or for someone --- it becomes apparent this is a two-way street between politicians wanting something and others wanting something from politicians.

WASTE AND FRAUD

We have heard about "Waste and Fraud," at least since Senator Proxmire's Golden Fleece Awards in 1975. Government Waste and Fraud will always be with us because they constitute someone's income.

Many politicians subscribe to the Keynesian notion that every dollar the government spends, wasted or not, results in $2.00 of economic activity. Nancy Pelosi said on the House floor, *"Unemployment insurance, the economists tell us, return $2 for every $1 that is put out there for unemployment insurance, it injects demand into the economy, it creates jobs to help reduce the deficit,"* Just imagine if everyone became unemployed, we'd all be twice as rich.

The federal government spent about $3.5 Trillion in 2012! Generally speaking, the more money spent the easier to get a handle on it. An analysis of campaign spending indicates that about 1/3 of campaign contributions by large corporations is divided between both parties as big business likes to hedge its bets.

Think solar panel company, Solyndra. It contributed $100,000 or more to President Obama's campaign and "coincidentally" received $535 million in taxpayer loan guarantees. Other corporations have benefited similarly under other Presidents. Some call it "Crony Capitalism." It would be more correct to call it "Crony Socialism."

I once walked into a business meeting without an appointment between a top Democrat and a top Republican in San Diego

They were sharing inside information on likely city council decisions to the advantage of their partnership and could care less about the ideology of those they supported, Democrats or Republicans.

Most Washington law firms purportedly have both Democrat and Republican sections. Why do you suppose that is?

Contrary to popular belief, many businessmen, particularly those running large corporations, are not supporters of free enterprise or defenders of Capitalism. They prefer privatization of their profits, government underwriting their losses and ever-increasing regulation of their competitors.

If you want to get the hell scared out of you sit in an elected body's "Executive Session" (legally secret). In one City of San Diego session, a councilman wanted to destroy a paramedic service for taking more than 5 minutes to respond to his mother's emergency. Another said the Gas & Electric Company had no property rights regarding an eminent domain "takings." He was elected and obligated to save the taxpayers money by paying no compensation, and a third wanted to double a cable TV company's Franchise Fee for some unstated slight. All three were Republicans.

POLITICIANS ONLY HALF THE PROBLEM

Winston Churchill thought the best argument against democracy was to have a 5-minute conversation with the average voter. He felt a democracy was the worst form of government except for all others.

I was stunned a few years ago to meet a young African-American mother and her father visiting from Alabama (average voters), who did not know who Bull Connor was, the Birmingham Police Commissioner.

In 1963, Connor unleashed fire hoses and police attack dogs on peaceful children marching for civil rights. You can Google the horrific photos under "Bull Connor." Is it possible that textbooks in the South have been purged of this unsavory historical fact?[1]

Younger generations who do not know their history, especially those who do not know Presidential candidate George Wallace and Bull Connor were Democrats and why Martin Luther King was a Republican, may very well be doomed to repeat it.

Condoleezza Rice explained that while growing up in the South it was the Democrats who refused to register her father to vote, something the Republicans did.

Democrats today will throw you off guard by telling you that President Richard Nixon got all the racists to leave the Democrat Party and join the Republicans as part of his "Southern Strategy." (A few did, most did not). They also contend that the Republicans who for years worked for civil rights and against segregation joined the Democrat Party. A very sweet fairy-tale to assuage the consciences of today's Democrats.

A lack of historical knowledge is not confined to American youths. Sixty percent of Austrians (average voters), in March 2013 said they want a "Strong Man" to lead their country and 40% think things were not all bad under Adolph Hitler.

I was flabbergasted years ago when a high school buddy married a girl from Germany and she told me one day, *"Hitler, Hitler, Hitler, in this country (the U.S.) you only tell about the bad things he did --- never about the schools and highways he built, or "the people's car."* Wow!

Joseph Stalin was born in the Russian Empire when Georgia was a part of it, where 45% of the people (average voters) still hold a positive attitude toward the former Soviet Leader. However, 39%, (average voters) do not even know who Stalin was.

There is a popular saying variously attributed to Edmund Burke, George Santayana and Winston Churchill, *"Those that fail to learn from history are doomed to repeat it."*

1. http://www.crmvet.org/images/imgbham.htm

Notes

Chapter 1

_____

_____

_____

_____

_____

_____

_____

_____

_____

_____

_____

_____

_____

_____

_____

_____

_____

_____

_____

_____

_____

_____

_____

_____

_____

_____

_____

_____

Chapter 2

Liberals and Conservatives Think Differently

"Scientists know now that there is, in human nature, a divide between what we sometimes call 'liberals' and 'conservatives."

--- Al Gore, January 30, 2013

Thomas Sowell opens his book, *A Conflict of Visions*, with *"A curious thing about political opinions is how often the same people line up on opposite sides of different issues."*

Sowell does not use the political words liberal and conservative to describe different visions, but uses the politically neutral terms "unconstrained" and "constrained." Terms to explain why invariably the same people are on one side or the other of minimum wage rates, gun control, the death penalty, right to life, government spending, taxes and oil drilling, etc.; most of which seem unconnected to each other.

In fact, "right to life" and the "death penalty" seem like opposites but actually go together like a horse and carriage.

The proponents of each vision, Sowell notes, *"have fundamentally different ideas of how the world works."*

The unconstrained (Liberals) share some conservative visions and the constrained (Conservatives) share some liberal visions. The unconstrained, however, are primarily concerned with "equality of results." They "feel" this is the only way to prove fairness, equality, and justice --- often stating, *"They are socially liberal but fiscally conservative."*

The constrained vision "believes" equal results are impossible without resorting to authoritarian rule and they advocate "equality of opportunity" for obtaining desirable results --- often stating this creates a *"fair field without favor."*

To liberals "intentions" are crucial. To conservatives intentions are irrelevant. To them it is "incentives" that are crucial.

25

Both visions want to improve social results; however, they interpret the meaning of words differently.

THE MEANING OF WORDS

Years ago, just after being freed, a seven-year Vietnam Prisoner of War spoke at a Board of Realtors luncheon on what impressed him most about his captors, The North Vietnamese. They felt they lived in a free country just as much if not more free than Americans.

Ho Chi Minh, after all, had proclaimed independence in 1945 writing, *"Nothing is more valuable than freedom and independence ... All men are born equal: the Creator has given us inviolable rights to life, liberty, and happiness!"* (Obviously, this is a contradiction in the meaning of these words within its Constitution that gives the state almost unlimited power).

Karl Marx taught that *"The theory of the Communists may be summed up in the single sentence: Abolition of private property."* Marx felt "independence" meant freedom from property, freedom from religion, freedom from profits and freedom from government.

Dr. Bernie Cordes, 1975 Chairman of the County Board of Public Welfare hung a 6-foot poster of Chairman Mao Zedong on his dining room wall. He told me that Red China had the answer to universal health care. Stuttering, I said. *"But, but, but what about the people's loss of freedom?"*

He said, *"So what?"* China's intentions for universal health care were all that counted, and the Chinese Communists had achieved it. Liberals are able to overlook the failure of or unintended consequences of many programs because they focus like a laser on "intentions."

When on the San Diego City Council I was so proud to cleverly wangle the hiring of 100 additional police officers, I met with the head of the POA (Police Union) to celebrate. Jack Pearson told me, *"Fred, we don't want more officers, we don't want two-man patrols, and we don't want shotguns. We want more money! Got it?"* I was crestfallen.

26

Jack was echoing the celebrated labor leader Samuel Gompers who said, *"We want more, and when it becomes more, we shall still want more! ... Show me the country that has no strikes and I'll show you the country in which there is no liberty."*

Abraham Lincoln, prior to Gompers noted, *"We all declare for liberty, but in using the same word, we do not mean the same thing."*

CHANGING THEIR STRIPES

Road to Damascus conversions are rare by either camp; however, after decades of criticizing it, conservatives eventually embraced FDR's Social Security. Responding to President Obama's State of the Union address Republican Senator Marco Rubio said, *"I would never support any changes to Medicare (Social Security) that would hurt seniors like my mother."*

In the other camp, Democrats, which for three-fourths of their party's history, were racists, anti-Semites, and KKK members responsible for untold lynching of Negroes, have made an earth shattering transformation, although Thomas Sowell writes that Democrats still treat *"Blacks as Mascots and Trophies."*

Nobel Laureate F.A. Hayek, one of the most honored proponents of individual liberty, interestingly, thought of himself like Milton Friedman, not as a conservative but a "Liberal" before the word liberal was preempted by "Progressives." Friedman said he opposed the "Draft and backed the legalization of drugs," and still I'm called a conservative. Both men preferred to be known as and called "Classical Liberals." Hayek, in *The Constitution of Liberty* has an interesting chapter on why he is not a conservative.

When you watch Fox News, the only major network that concedes there actually are legitimate conservative and liberal viewpoints on many subjects, the split screen will show two protagonists speaking right past each other seldom hearing, connecting or directly answering the other. They smile, grin, scowl, and appeal to likeminded listeners and seemingly write off those in the broad undecided middle.

Facts, in most cases are not persuasive to either side. Sowell points out that, *"Theories can be devastated by facts but can never be proved to be correct by facts."*

237 YEARS OF LIBERALS V. CONSERVATIVES (since 1776)

The divide is not new. The constrained view has been represented by Adam Smith (Inquiry into the Wealth of Nations, 1776), James Madison (U.S. Constitution, adopted 1789), Friedrich Hayek (The Road to Serfdom, 1944), Ludwig von Mises (Human Action, 1949), and Milton Friedman (Capitalism & Freedom, 1976).

The unconstrained view has been represented by William Godwin (Enquiry Concerning Political Justice, 1793), Thomas Paine, Jean-Jacque Rousseau, John Rawls (A Theory of Justice, 1971), John Kenneth Galbraith (The Affluent Society 1998), and Nobel Laureate Paul Krugman (The Conscience of a Liberal, 2007).

Liberal Professor Louis Michael Seidman said in early 2013 on 60 Minutes, *"Suppose that Barack Obama really wasn't a natural-born citizen. So what? Constitutional obedience has a pernicious impact on our political culture."* The Constitution to liberals can be both, "an irrelevant relic" to be ignored or "living document" interpreted at will. The Constitution means whatever they say it means.

Human nature and the state of mankind have been the same for eons, short, nasty and brutish. To conservatives the Constitution sets forth fundamental principles that both limits the government more than any government has ever been limited and at the same time frees mankind, frees the common people. This has resulted in an unprecedented era of growth and development.

More human progress has been made since 1789 than in all previous recorded history. The Constitution is the most important political document ever written and sadly, conservatives recognize it is not a living but a dying document.

IGNORANCE IN GOVERNMENT

Friedrich Hayek in *The Constitution of Liberty* cites The Harvard Business Review.

"Consider for a moment that any one person can only know a fraction of what is going on around him. Much of what that person believes will be false rather than true . . . At any given time, vastly more is not known than is known . . . It seems possible, then, in organizing into a hierarchy of authority for the purpose of increasing efficiency, we may really be institutionalizing ignorance."

Hayek elaborates, *"The case for individual freedom rests chiefly on the recognition of the inevitable ignorance of all of us concerning a great many of the factors on which the achievement of our ends and welfare depends. . . . It is because every individual knows so little and, in particular, because we rarely know which of us knows best that we trust the independent and competitive efforts of many to induce the emergence of what we shall want when we see it."*

Leonard Read (The Foundation for Economic Education) put it more succinctly, *"There is wisdom in the free market a trillion times greater than within any discrete group no matter how smart each individual."* (Whether they are intellectuals or politicians.)

INDIVIDUALISM V. THE COMMON GOOD

In some respects, this is a contest between the "rugged individualism" of the constrained vision and the unconstrained vision of the "public good, or good of society." The latter encompass liberals or Democrats acting as self-appointed surrogates with superior wisdom speaking for not only the benighted poor, hungry, and downtrodden, but self-appointed surrogates claiming to speak for "everybody."

However, since no one can go out and talk to *"society"* the constrained view maintains that for something to be for society, the people, or the public good, all-inclusive terms, it would have to be for the good of every man, woman and child.

It's hard to name anything liberal or conservative meeting that criterion. Liberals frequently use the terms *"fair"* or "for the children" and opinions with which they disagree are dismissed as *"simplistic,"* or from *"the best minds of the 19th century."*

Former Democrat, Ronald Reagan retorted, *"They're wrong. I have 18th-century ideas. I learned them from our founders."*

With rare exceptions, prominent conservatives have been more generous in their opinions of adversaries, attributing their visions as misguided or uninformed. Hayek in his remarkably influential book, **The Road to Serfdom,** characterized his adversaries as *"single minded idealists,"* and *"whose sincerity and disinterestedness are above suspicion."* Many of his adversaries nonetheless think Hayek a moral leper.

Paul Krugman, wrote in his New York Times column, *"[Mitt Romney and Paul Ryan] want to expose many Americans to financial insecurity, and let some of them die, so that a handful of already wealthy people can have a higher after-tax income."* ABC News' David Chalian, *"[Ann and Mitt Romney] ... are happy to have a party with black people drowning."* Allison Yarrow on the Newsweek/Daily Beat Web show, *"[Dick Cheney] may be one of the most evil people in the world."*

Liberals consider their adversaries evil with malice towards all while wishing "heart attacks or death" on conservatives such as Rush Limbaugh and Dick Cheney. According to liberals, when conservatives use the words, "apartment, Chicago, illegal, golf, law and order, food-stamp President" and "states' rights," they are using code words for racist hate speech.

Bill Maher and Howard Stern call Sarah Palin and Michele Bachman the C-word. Mike Malloy said, *"[Dick] Cheney is a murderer. He's a killer. He's a torturer. He is evil personified! He is a walking mass of horror and when he's gone, this planet will be cleaner!"* No code words here!

When minorities such as Colin Powell, Condoleezza Rice, and Clarence Thomas are promoted to high positions, Republicans get no credit because they merited promotions. Under Rawls, **Theory of Justice,** as

President Obama might say, they "did not earn it," they were "born" with exceptional abilities (or high IQs) and their emoluments are not fair.

"Inequalities of wealth and authority are just and fair only if they result in compensating... the least advantaged of society... [The greater] injustice is the greater benefits earned by a few"   ---John Rawls

A LIBERAL OR CONSERVATIVE? THAT IS THE QUESTION

What do Bill Clinton, Ronald Reagan, Sarah Palin and Barack Obama have in common? They emote! They exude emotions and have a charisma that cannot be taught or learned; otherwise, campaign consultants would be turning out similar personas by the thousands. It's not what they say but how they make you feel --- that causes their devotees to overlook any flaws.

Feelings may also apply to issues. Few voters can articulate why they are for or against "Same-sex Marriages" but nearly everyone can tell you if they "feel" positive or negative. Or think of how your favorite songs make you "feel" while not hearing what the words say.

The liberal New York Times made an interestingly observation in 2008, *"The upshot is that Democrats, who speak passionately about the hungry and homeless, personally fork over less money (30% to 50% less) to charity than Republicans — the ones who try to cut health insurance for children."*

Conservatives like to point out that liberals love humanity, but hate people. Abortion is only one example. Regarding compassion, liberals get so-called "Two-fers:" One is credit for their government funded compassion and two, their compassion is cost free to them.

Both liberals and conservatives, by different names, support "Regulated Capitalism" as an economic system. For politicians, Democrat or Republican, being either for or against taxes and regulations is a never-ending source of campaign contributions for both political parties.

2. http://www.nytimes.com/2008/12/21/opinion/21kristof.html

Regardless of the results stemming from the unconstrained and constrained visions, President Obama in 2012 (like nearly all Presidents) received less than 1/3 of the support from those legally "eligible to vote," (the VEP/Voter Eligible Population).

This, by no measure, is a legitimate mandate. Additionally, for over 2 decades, about twice as many Americans have claimed to be conservatives as liberals, 46% to 20% in 2012, according to a Gallup Poll. Which vision is most persuasive?

SUMMARIZED IN THREE QUOTES:

"To understand the working of American politics, you have to understand this fundamental law: Conservatives think liberals are stupid. Liberals think conservatives are evil." Charles Krauthammer

"Conservatives and liberals may have one less thing in common: neurology. ProCon.org has gathered 13 peer-reviewed studies of behavioral and neurological studies and has come to the conclusion that differences between Republicans and Democrats are more than skin-deep. Democrats had larger anterior cingulate cortexes, which are associated with tolerance to uncertainty, while Republicans had larger right amygdalas, which are associated with sensitivity to fear." Conservatives and Liberals Have Different Brains, Studies Show – ABC World News with Diane Sawyer, September 3, 2012, cited by Al Gore.

"If you're not Liberal when you're 25, you have no heart. If you're not Conservative when you're 35, you have no brain."

Notes

Chapter 2

Chapter 3

Gun ignorance

"Americans have the right and advantage of being armed"

-James Madison

When it comes to gun violence, we only know a fraction of what there is to know, vastly more is unknown than known, and most of what we know is wrong. Opportunists find in incomprehensible, unexplainable tragedies an opportunity to raise money and promote their agendas on firearms.

To Gunaphobes and gunaphiles alike, guns are a religion. Their faiths are staked out. Facts won't alter the perceptions of either side.

A 2007 study published by Harvard provides counterintuitive evidence to both conservatives and liberals using astonishing data from 150 footnoted sources. The study in Volume 30, No. 2 of the Harvard Journal of Law & Public Policy (Page 649-694) sets out to answer the question in its title: "Would Banning Firearms Reduce Murder and Suicide? A Review of International and Some Domestic Evidence."[3]

ORIGINS OF THE SECOND AMENDMENT

First, let's look at the origin of the Second Amendment's "right to bear arms." In 1770, British soldiers fired on unarmed American civilians in what became known as the Boston Massacre, a prelude to the Second Amendment being adopted in 1791.

To paraphrase James Madison in The Federalist, No. 46, *"Americans [have] the right and advantage of being armed — unlike citizens of other countries whose governments are afraid to trust the people with arms."*

Moreover, incorrectly attributed to Thomas Jefferson, but to the point, *"The strongest reason for the people to retain the right to keep and bear arms is, as a last resort, to protect themselves against tyranny in government."*

3. http://www.law.harvard.edu/students/orgs/jlpp/Vol30_No2_KatesMauseronline.pdf

The Bill of Rights is first and foremost about protecting people not from guns, but from government.

Suffice to say that if the right to bear arms, freedom of the press and religion were not codified in the U.S. Constitution America would likely have evolved into a far different country. One only need look to countries today where firearms are banned, that have state controlled media or theocracies.

Their leaders, like ours, claim to only want the best for their people without "checks and balances" and without acknowledging that "Power corrupts."

89 COUNTRIES HAVE HIGHER MURDER RATES THAN U.S.

A United Nations 2010 chart lists the U.S. as having a murder rate of 5.22 per 100,000 people. The world average homicide rate: 9.63 per 100,000.

In comparing the United States and Europe, it is interesting that in the past two decades, Europe has had as many multiple-victim shootings as the United States, with four of the 10 worst K-12 killings in Europe. The most killed worldwide were in Beslan, Russia (386). Among the 10 worst mass school killings are Virginia Tech (32); Netiv Meir elementary school in Ma'alot, Israel (26); Dunblane Primary School in Dunblane, Scotland (17); Gutenberg-Gymnasium in Erfurt, Germany (16); University of Texas in Austin (16); École Polytechnique in Montreal (14); Columbine High School in Columbine, Colo. (13); and a Catholic elementary school in Cologne, Germany (10). This in spite of the fact that most European countries have stricter gun laws than the United States, which the U.S. media tend to ignore.

The worst K-12 school murders in the United States happened May 18, 1927, in Bath, Mich., when 44 were killed and 58 wounded **by dynamite** set off by a former school board member. (The 77 killed in Norway are not on the school list, because they were killed at a summer camp.)

The "per capita murder rate *overall* is only half as frequent in the United States as in several other nations where *gun* murder is rarer, but murder

35

by strangling, stabbing, or beating is much more frequent," according to the Harvard Journal of Law & Public Policy, Page 663.

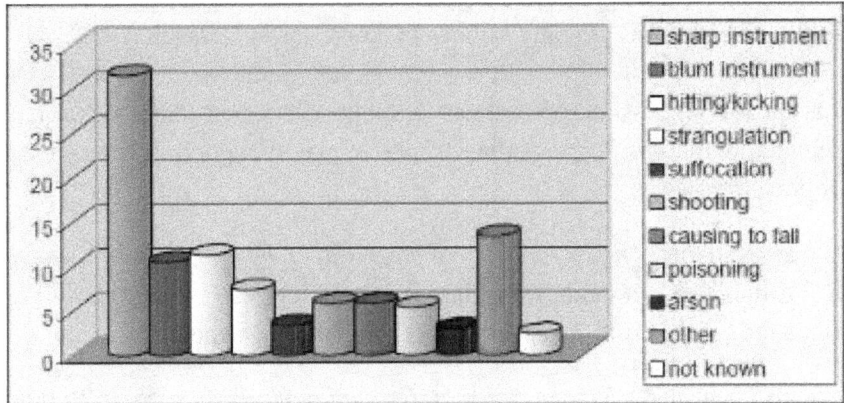

Figure 1

A 2003 study by the Home Office and Scotland Yard noted that 33% of homicides in the United Kingdom between 1979 and 1998 were more often committed with knives (and sharp objects) versus 5% with guns --- about six times as many killings by knives as by guns.

Figure 1. Method of killing (percentages), homicides in England and Wales, 1995-1999 Combined. [4]

Japan, with nearly total gun control has amongst the lowest murder rates per 100,000 people. But we would have to abolish our Bill of Rights and Constitution to do what Japan does with routine police inspections of homes. Mexico with strict controls on firearms, and with 120,000 murders since 2006, has a murder rate with guns 5 times higher than the U.S. (Union-Tribune 3/19/13).

Switzerland and Israel have relatively high gun ownership rates and below world average murder rates. Switzerland does not have a standing army and nearly all men between 20 and 30 are conscripted into the militia. Its exceptionally low murder rate is similar to Japan's validating the bumper sticker: "People, not guns, kill people."

4.http://webarchive.nationalarchives.gov.uk/ 20110220105210/rds.homeoffice.gov.uk / rds / pdfs2 / rdsolr0103.pdf

A 2004 RAND study in San Diego found that semiautomatic assault rifles (contrary to the popular belief of politicians) are rarely used in homicides — only twice (3 percent of the time) in 59 murders. And, there are four times as many killings by knives as by "assault rifles."

Except for single-shot, or shotgun, virtually every non-military gun is a semiautomatic. While preventing their sale may feel good, it is an empty political gesture.

We are told that, *"If just one life can be saved by banning guns it's worth it."* If that's true, wouldn't banning cars and bicycles save far more lives since far more people are killed by cars and bicycle accidents than guns?

We also hear that *"No one needs a 16 round ammunition clip."* Well no one needs a car that can go 100 miles per hour, or needs a micro-wave oven or hundreds of other things.

Additionally, Secret Service agents claim they can change 10-round clips in less than one and a half seconds, some in a second. It is not how many rounds you have but the number that assailants have.

In the April 2013 shootout with the two Boston Marathon Bombers, the police reported they fired 200 rounds killing only one of the terrorists. That is 200 rounds by experts trained in firearms.

Another RAND study of 2,190 criminals found that the average "career criminal" commits 187 to 287 crimes a year, which explains why the crime rate has fallen so much with a record number of criminals now in prison.

These criminals confess they avoid people and places where there is likely to be a defensive gun.

"Guns in private hands are used 2.5 million times each year to prevent crime, or 6,849 every day, including rapes, aggravated assaults, and kidnapping. The number of innocent children protected by guns far outweighs the number hurt by guns." Gary Kleck, Criminologist, Florida State University.

What about the Gun Show loophole? The Bureau of Justice Statistics NCJ 189369, in a Survey of Inmates in State & Federal Correctional Facilities on Firearm Use by Offenders, reported that 0.7 percent of criminals obtained their guns from gun shows in 1997 and 0.6 percent from gun shows in1991.[5]

Fortunately, as guns have become cheaper and more available over the centuries the worldwide murder rate, with occasional upticks, has been falling.

Between 1990 and 2010, the FBI reported that homicides in New York dropped 76 percent, down 70 percent in Los Angeles and 49 percent in Chicago. Hollywood, as you might expect, supports more gun control to deflect scrutiny for promoting a gun violence culture through movies, TV and video games.

To claim movies, TV and video games do not influence behavior is to say that the Bible, pornography and advertising do not influence people.

Undoubtedly mental illness is a factor in mass killings, but in a free society, the best we can hope is to identify in advance the very few mentally ill that go berserk.

Despite the 2012 tragedy at Newtown, Connecticut (26 killed), schools nationwide are incredibly safe and killings incredibly rare. It was reported, however, that the shooter Adam Lanza was taking medication. What medication was he on?

The Adverse Events Reporting System for drug side effects listed 12,755 reports of psychiatric medications relating to violence between 2004 and 2011. Included were 14 school shootings and 10 murders on page 3, with a total of 102 dead. One of the shooters at Columbine, Eric Harris, was on the antidepressant drug, Luvox.[6]

5. http://webcache.googleusercontent.com/search?q=cache:0yZHPNnRWqMJ:news.findlaw.com/hdo
cs/docs/doj/offfirearmuse1101rpt.pdf+Caroline+Wolf+Harlow,+%EF%BF%BD%EF%BF%BD%E
F%BF%BDFirearm+Use+by+Offenders,%EF%BF%BD%EF%BF%BD%EF%BF%BD+Bureau+
o +Justice+Statistics,+U.S.+Department+of+Justice,+Nov.+2001&hl=en&gl=us
6. http://www.cchrint.org/2013/04/17/are-psychotropic-drugs-actually-linked-to-mass-shootings/

YOU ARE 11-TIMES MORE LIKELY TO BE ACCIDENTLY SHOT BY A POLICEMAN THAN AN ARMED CITIZEN

What about accidental gun deaths? In the November 15, 1993 issue of Newsweek, George Will reported that police are 5 times more likely than a civilian to shoot an innocent person by mistake. Don't think that just because the police are trained in the use of firearms that they are less likely to kill an innocent person.

It gets worse. A University of Chicago Study revealed that in 1993 approximately 700,000 police killed 330 innocent individuals, while approximately 250,000,000 private citizens only killed 30 innocent people. Policemen accidentally killed 11 times as many people. In 2007, there were 613 fatal firearm accidents in the U.S. This was 0.5% of 123,706 fatal accidents that year.

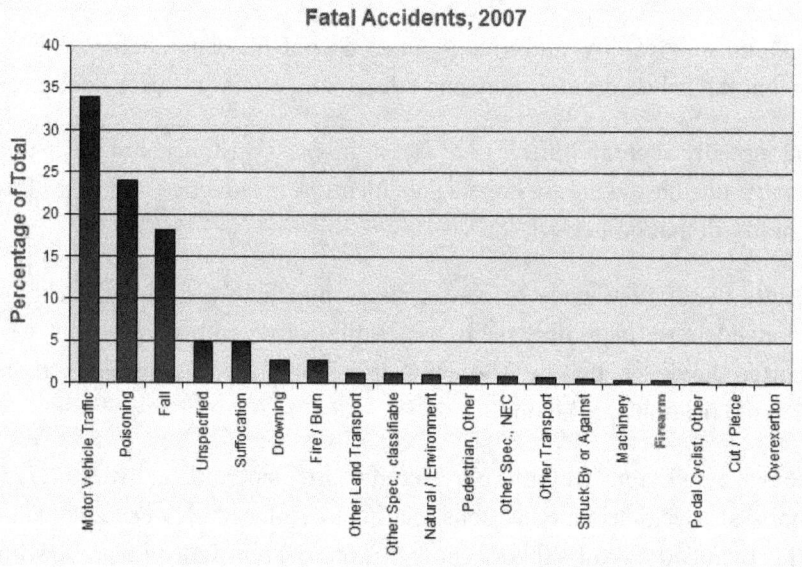

Source: Courtesy of http://www.justfacts.com/guncontrol.asp

We hear a lot about children killed by guns. If less than 18 years of age you're considered a child (sometimes up to 26) and many children in this category of gun deaths die in drug related activity or "Juvenile Gang Killings" committed by other children particularly of 15-24 age. Both Boston Bombers were called kids repeatedly in news reports while acknowledging one was 19 and the other 26.

Notes

Chapter 3

Chapter 4

Death penalty debate nonsense on stilts

"I would have done it again"
(After killing 77 people) --- Anders Breivik

My father was shot twice in the chest during a 1976 holdup in Dallas. The inside job was perpetrated by a former employee on parole for murder.

He was caught some six months later, and the police reported that his plan was to rob and kill my stepmother, the business manager, and any witnesses. My father was a witness that fateful day. Had the perpetrator been executed when convicted of his first homicide, no one else could ever have been put at risk by this parolee.

The undeniable fact ignored by Betsey Stevenson and Justin Wolfers in a Bloomberg column "Death penalty debate needs reality check" (June 15, 2012) is that murderers who are executed can never murder again. Therefore, the death penalty is a proven deterrent and not debatable.

As a Catholic, I have always considered those opposed to the death penalty as having very little respect for human life, those people who view other humans as mere ciphers on an obituary page.

You can take another's life according to them and the worst penalty you can get is life in prison (which under the law does not necessarily mean the remainder of your life). A life sentence, which varies from state to state, generally means 20 or more years in prison before parole is possible and often means serving only 14 years if commuted.

The ludicrous explanation that it is society's fault and not the perpetrators of crime is absurd. What those who make the claim are saying is that "society," the people who do not commit crimes, are the ones who are really responsible for whatever crime occurs. Are we really supposed to take these people seriously?

Someone can take another's life, or kill 77 people in Norway July 22, 2011, and the harshest punishment dished out is to be clothed, fed and imprisoned "for life," an imprisonment as noted above not always for the remainder of the killer's life.

Norwegian Anders Behring Breivik said in court in 2012, *"I would have done it again."* For killing 77 people his maximum sentence allowed under the law is 21 years, or 3.3 months for each life. Norwegians seem to think this makes them an enlightened and civilized society.

Undoubtedly, some innocent people have been executed. However, if the only way of ensuring that no miscarriage of justice is ever committed, that *"it is better to let 10 guilty people go free rather than punish one innocent person,"* then we would have to let everyone out of prison and close them all.

In summary: Anyone committing first-degree murder forfeits his own right to life. By depriving others of their lives, murderers must forfeit their own life. Whether the death penalty acts as a deterrent in the opinion of academics is beside the point. At least the killer cannot kill again.

Everyone can agree at the very minimum no person should ever be put to death based exclusively on "circumstantial" evidence. Unquestionably, every effort must be extended to ensure no person is unjustly executed, which is a lot different from saying no one must ever be executed by eliminating the Death Penalty.

The innocent are innocent; the guilty are guilty. The two distinctions should not be cleverly conflated or confused.

The Bible acknowledges, *"Whoever sheds man's blood, his blood will be shed by man, for God made man in his own image."*

— Genesis 9:6

Notes

Chapter 4

Chapter 5

Bread and Circuses – Is the 'Tea Party' rooted in ancient Rome?

"Our lives begin to end the day we become silent on things that matter."
---Martin Luther King

The world is moved by men of principle. Sad to say, many people fear men of principle. Those fearing men and women who stand for something often ridicule, laugh at, and tear them down. Most people, too often it seems, prefer argumentum ad populum, or populism.

In short, what's in it for me, damn the torpedoes and full speed ahead with unprecedented government spending. It applies to manipulators and the manipulated.

Originally, the term "Bread and Circuses" meant the manner in which the government in Ancient Rome pacified the populace. Today it is a metaphor for pacifying the general population to distract them from the mess politicians are making of the economy.

In Ancient Rome, Tiberius Gracchus tried to implement an agrarian reform law that took lands captured from rich enemies and redistributed it to the peasants.

After his assassination, he was followed by his younger brother Gaius Gracchus. In the family tradition, Gaius opened public granaries for whoever was willing to stand in line, grain to be paid for --- by the rich.

Gaius too was assassinated. When Julius Caesar came to power he implemented welfare reform, cutting the relief rolls by an estimated 150,000 or by about one-half and he too was assassinated. The public granaries are the bread part of Bread and Circuses.

The circuses took place in the Coliseum in Rome, which my wife and I visited a few years ago. Looking down upon the floor you couldn't help see in your mind's eye the games that occurred there; imagine Spartacus, the Circus Maximus, Ben-Hur, imagine the Gladiators' quarters and written in Latin on the walls: Lions 10, Christians zero.

Have you ever wondered why the Roman circuses ended --- in that Coliseum where men would fight men --- men would fight animals --- combat to the death? Where the crowds ultimately would determine who lived or died with a thumbs up or thumbs down? Well, the end of the games can be traced to "One Man of Principle." One man with courage makes a majority, as the saying goes.

Robert LeFevre gives his rendition of the story about the Asiatic monk, Telemachus, on his first trip to Rome in the fifth century. *"It was a holiday in the city by the Tiber. Men and women dressed in their brightest and best, swarmed into the Coliseum for one of those brilliant, bloody spectacles which excited the emotions of ... a jaded people."*

Telemachus found a seat in the lowest tier next to the arena wall. The crowd of 80,000 roared approval as the column of men marched into the arena below Caesar's royal box. *"Giving the Roman salute -- sword raised upward, slapped smartly across the chest -- the gladiators shouted in unison, 'We who are about to die salute you!'"*

Telemachus expected what today would be a NFL football game with pomp and circumstance, not a game to the death with swords and tridents. But the meaning of that salute was clear to him making him want to throw up. Being Christian, he could not sit quietly as gladiators tried to mutilate and decapitate each other. His faith taught him that killing a man for amusement is wrong.

Without thinking he vaulted over the wall and ran to the place between the gladiators and the emperor. *"In the name of Christ: Stop!"* The crowd stared in disbelief. The arrogance -- trying to interfere with their fun and games! On second thought maybe he's a paid clown, part of the pageant. Loud laughter rang out among the throng. *"This guy is hysterical."*

Telemachus ran between two rows of gladiators facing each other who if lost, would die at the pleasure of the crowd. As loud as he could Telemachus yelled: *"Stop this unspeakable act! Right now: Stop!"* A gladiator knocked him off his feet. The crowd laughed even louder.

Telemachus jumped up and tried to disarm the gladiator. This clown was serious. From the stands: *"Run him through!"* rang out. A blade flashed and Telemachus fell to his knees --- his blood oozing dark red in the sand beneath him. Then the clanging of steel --- the games began.

Then something odd happened. From one of the furthest seats at the top of the arena one man rose hardly noticed and left. Those seated next to him nodded to each other, *"let's go."* The sickening feeling spread rapidly. Then by the tens, hundreds and thousands, people quietly filed out of the Coliseum.

The spectacle went on but a pall fell upon those who remained perhaps dawning on them what Martin Luther King, Jr. would describe some 16 centuries later, *"Our lives begin to end the day we become silent about things that matter."*

The beginning of the end of the annual slaughter of thousands was at hand -- the end of the government's ability to divert the people's attention from the mess it had made of Roman lives, their economy and culture.

More circuses were organized with ever fewer attending. Today the Coliseum is empty -- standing in eerie silence. One man of principle defied Caesar -- one man of courage defied a multitude of 80,000 and became a majority. (The Catholic Church, attributing the sudden end of the games in 404 A.D. to Telemachus, canonized him a saint. He died for his beliefs. But the principle had been established.)

Today, men and women of principle look at the mess our government is making of the economy and spontaneously are joining the TEA (Taxed Enough Already) Party. They are being ridiculed, laughed at, and torn down all across the land. Seeing Congressmen on TV deliberately mocking our Constitution, they are standing up and crying out: *Stop!*

Notes

Chapter 5

Chapter 6

Why Is America Rich?

"You can have everything you want in life if you provide enough people everything they want."   ---Zig Ziglar

Because we Americans are richer today in more ways than were kings and queens, princes and potentates, throughout most of history, we often forget that America is an historical aberration.

In "Capitalism & Freedom," Milton Friedman reminds us *"The typical state of mankind is tyranny, servitude and misery."* In addition, in most times and most countries your status was fixed from birth until the day you died.

Imagine 200 years ago the richest men on earth never having access to antibiotics, television, telephones, automobiles, computers, air-conditioning, air travel, and a hundred other miracles available today to most secretaries and gardeners for less than a month's wages.

Many Americans assume the reason they enjoy higher wages than other people in other countries is because they're more educated, more skilled, or through their own merit (or union membership). A little travel to other countries and they would discover otherwise.

For example, a worker who migrates from, say Iraq -- such as my neighbor Nihad -- finds he can soon realize the wage rates common here, but if he goes back to Baghdad, what he learned here will not enable him to earn more than his fellow countrymen doing the same job. Nor can the reason be explained that businessmen and entrepreneurs in Iraq are inferior.

Iraq's lower wages are not due to inferiority or ignorance. They are due to less savings, less capital accumulation and fewer rich people --- rich people with a propensity to save and invest in capital goods, machinery, and equipment, etc. Investment capital is what enables workers here to produce more units of output for each hour worked.

Obviously a man with a D-8 tractor is more productive than a dozen men with shovels, with a chainsaw more than with a hand saw, with a spray-gun than with a paintbrush (all tools produced through profits, savings and investments).

Poor countries do have rich people but absent well-defined property rights and laws to protect them, they prefer not to invest where it's risky. Think of Venezuela when Hugo Chavez, was nationalizing one company after another and investors were fleeing the country. (See: Why Capitalism Triumphs in the West and Fails Everywhere Else by Hernando de Soto.[7]

If the United States in its early years had the same regulations and progressive taxation as now it could never have developed to the degree we see today. Had not the great railroads, canals and factories been built before the advent of progressive taxation beginning with the income tax in 1913 the degree of development, wealth and our standard of living would have been much slower.

Rich people only consume a portion of what they earn and most reinvest the bulk of their money to earn more. When fewer become rich there's less surplus capital to invest, less money to create new factories, machinery and equipment, and less money to replace existing things as they wear out --- which lead to fewer jobs.

It's true higher taxes can lead to less inequality of income, however, hard as it may be for some to accept, when government redistributes wealth eventually everyone, rich and poor – become poorer.

It's reported that U.S. capital stock is shrinking for the first time and more capital is being invested in China and emerging countries resulting in their faster growth in per capita incomes despite their long moribund economies due to government "Central Planning."

We leave it to those who claim it's natural resources that make a country rich to explain Japan, Hong Kong and Singapore's extraordinarily high per capita incomes or you can simply review The Ultimate Resource2.[8]

7. http://www.amazon.com / Mystery-Capital-Capitali / dp / 0465016154
8. http://press.princeton.edu/chapters/s5941.html

INEQUALITY IS ESSENTIAL TO A FREE MARKET

"It is not from the benevolence of the butcher, the brewer or the baker, that we expect our dinner, but from their regard to their own self-interest."   ---The Wealth of Nations, Adam Smith

Motivational speaker Zig Ziglar added: *"You can have everything you want in life if you provide enough people everything they want."*

For some reason a few people get all worked up over inequalities of income in society. Professor Ludwig von Mises, in his magisterial "Human Action," contended: *"The inequality of incomes and wealth is an inherent feature of the market economy. Its elimination would entirely destroy the market economy.*

What those people who ask for equality have in mind is always an increase in their own power to consume. In endorsing the principle of equality as a political postulate nobody wants to share his own income with those who have less.

When the American wage earner refers to equality, he means that the dividends of the stockholders should be given to him. He does not suggest a curtailment of his own income for the benefit of 95 percent of the earth's population whose income is lower than his."

Inequality of income is indispensable to progress. An increasing accumulation of capital relative to an increasing population is the only way to bring about technological improvements, bring about a greater supply of equipment, machinery and tools per capita and bring increased wages and therefore a higher standard of living.

Mises maintains, *"The crux of the issue lies precisely in the operation of selfishness. Under the system of inequality this selfishness impels a man to save and always to invest his savings in such a way as to fill best the most urgent needs of the consumers. Under a system of equality this motive fades."*

If all it took to raise wages was a union strike, or laws decreeing a higher minimum wage and guaranteed annual income, then all countries would follow Zimbabwe. All Zimbabweans are billionaires and yet 85 percent of its billionaires live below its poverty level according to the Zimbabwe Congress of Trade Unions. Even I would be a billionaire when in Zimbabwe and have the cash to prove it by owning the "actual" note below.

Specimen   Actual

The Zimbabwe government taxes, spends, promises, and then prints money in billion-dollar notes to pay for its promises. Upon its 1980 independence, the Zimbabwe dollar for a few years was worth more than the U.S. dollar.

Merely having money, however, doesn't necessarily make one rich. What will your money buy? A standard of living depends upon how many hours of work it takes to buy food, clothing, shelter, etc., --- how productive you are. How much people are willing to pay for what you produce? In reality, it's consumers who establish your pay.

Wealth must be created anew everyday --- food, clothing, shelter. Politicians kid themselves if they think the people who create wealth will continue doing so if their wealth is redistributed through some utopian dream of "Social Justice," or changing the Commandment to *"Thou shall not steal -- except in the name of the poor."*

Wealth is earned --- not distributed. America is rich because it was founded on the principles of private property ownership, a free market economy, and a government more limited than any previous government in history. Rich because more money is invested in infrastructure, factories, machinery and technology, than in other countries while its culture eschews sloth, envy and covetousness.

Notes

Chapter 6

_____

_____

_____

_____

_____

_____

_____

_____

_____

_____

_____

_____

_____

_____

_____

_____

_____

_____

_____

_____

_____

_____

_____

_____

_____

_____

_____

_____

_____

Chapter 7

Media Ignore Individuals in Gap between Rich and Poor

"I've been rich and I've been poor, and rich is better" - Mae West

Whenever billionaire Bill Gates walks into McDonald's, statistically the "average income" of all present increases to more than $1 billion, despite no one actually being richer or poorer because of Gates presence.

Intentionally or not, using misleading statistical categories is how the media (including Pew Research) portray a growing gap between rich and poor. People like Gates, Warren Buffett and Steve Jobs skew enormously the "average income" of those in the top 20%, top 10%, top 5% and top 1% of all income earners.

Typically, when comparing rich and poor, it is categories that are compared, not individuals. You may, as an individual, become rich the year you sell a business, farm or real estate, but it doesn't mean you will be rich the following year.

The New York Times, The Washington Post and Newsweek report the gap between rich and poor is growing, but they don't tell you the top 1, 5, 10, and 20 percent are "statistical categories" with changing membership each year and significant changes over a 10-year period.

After joining even the top 1 percent, people within the group, such as billionaire Bernie Madoff, movie stars and business moguls, may see their income and wealth decline precipitously in succeeding years.

For example, 86 percent of the Fortune 500 companies in 1959 were either gone or were no longer in the top 500 companies in 2009, according to University of Michigan (Flint) economics professor Mark Perry. Undoubtedly, as a result, their top executives also suffered decreases in their incomes.

The IRS placed you in the top 10 percent in 2009 if your adjusted gross income was more than $113,799. What happens to people individually in a given category is not the same as what happens to the category as a whole.

People move up and down yearly in the top 1 percent and the other categories. In Reason Magazine's February, 2012 issue, Veronique de Rugy shows that of 675,000 millionaires in 1999, only 38,000 remained in 2007.

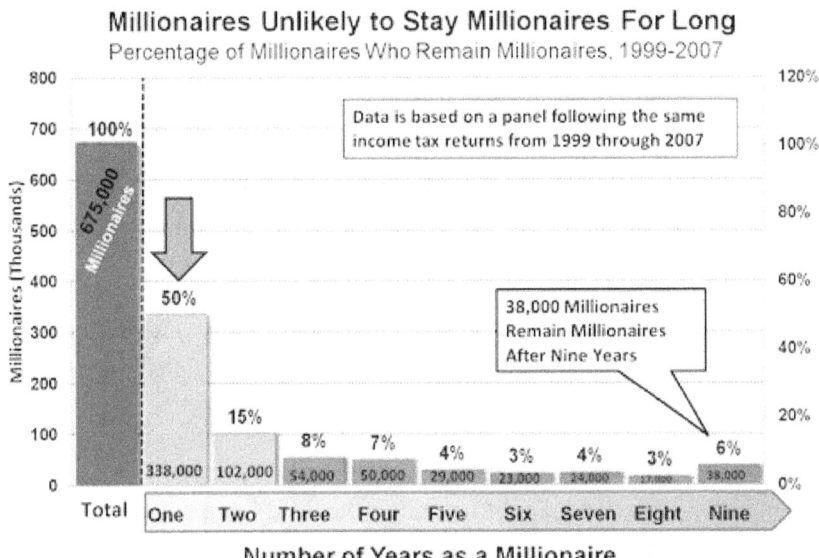

Millionaires Unlikely to Stay Millionaires For Long
Percentage of Millionaires Who Remain Millionaires, 1999-2007

Data is based on a panel following the same income tax returns from 1999 through 2007

38,000 Millionaires Remain Millionaires After Nine Years

Number of Years as a Millionaire

Source: Tax Foundation, Internal Revenue Service
Produced by Veronique de Rugy, Mercatus Center at George Mason University

Source: Courtesy of Veronique de Rugy

Numerous columnists tell us how the wealthy are under-taxed, even though the top 3 percent of income earners pay more personal income taxes than the other 97 percent, according to an August 2011 Wall Street Journal editorial citing the IRS.

Former President George W. Bush and the Republicans are accused of making their rich friends richer by giving them tax cuts. But tax cuts don't give anybody anything. Tax cuts simply allow people to keep more of what they work for and earn.

Those who say tax cuts "cost" the government X dollars of revenue are in effect, saying, all your income belongs to the government and anything less than 100% is a tax loophole. The government doesn't own us or our income, despite what some politicians think, and we certainly are not slaves of the government.

While it is true mathematically that the gap between the highest income category as a group and the lowest group is increasing, individuals tell a different story. Only by conflating separate sets of facts does the gap appear to be increasing.

In his book, "The Thomas Sowell Reader," professor Sowell, citing the IRS, points out the real incomes of those in the bottom quintile in 1996 rose 91 percent by 2005 while those in the top quintile rose by only 10 percent during the same period. *"And the incomes of those in the very top 5 percent and top 1 percent actually declined."*

Sowell writes that real flesh-and-blood human beings move from one statistical category to another over time, emphasizing that individuals should not be confused with categories or quintiles.

About half of all workers receiving the minimum wage are 16 to 24 years old, and of course they cannot remain in the 16-24 age category forever. As one cohort moves up in income, another cohort of young people assumes its position, ensuring that as long as one definition of poor is the bottom 10 or 20 percent, wrote Sowell, *"The poor will always be with us."*

Most of us can relate by looking at our personal income when graduating from high school or college to our peak earning years to what we expect in retirement, as we move up and then down the income ladder.

People who begin working at minimum wage typically experience the highest percentage increase in incomes over their first 10 years because it's far easier to double $8 per hour than to double Bill Gates' millions per hour. Bureau of Labor Statistics reports of those starting out only 1% receive the minimum wage for over 3 years.

Notes

Chapter 7

Chapter 8

Increasing Minimum Wage Would Generate Adverse Results

"If we started in 1960 ... then the minimum wage today would be about
$22 an hour"   ---Sen. Elizabeth Warren

President Obama has called for raising the minimum wage, or "learning wage," to $9.00 while declaring even this is not enough to live on.

If people can't survive on $9.00 per hour, why the hypocrisy? Why not raise it to $22 per hour as Senator Elizabeth Warren suggests or the $35 per hour the New York labor unions are advocating?

Low skilled workers who receive minimum wages comprise only 4.7% of hourly workers, according to the Bureau of Labor Statistics (2012). In 2004, less than 1 percent of all wage earners earned the minimum wage after three years.[9]

The Department of Labor reports one-tenth of those receiving the minimum wage were heads of families and qualified for Earned Income Tax Credits to supplement their wages.

The primary beneficiaries of minimum wage increases are not the 4.7% but those ratcheted above the new minimum wage that will get a step up in pay grade, and those with Union contracts stipulating increases whenever the minimum wage (learning wage) increases.

My very first job paid less than minimum wage. My boss thought I should first learn to show up for work on time and docked me when I didn't. He also insisted I learn to show up the day after payday when my buddies wanted to go to the beach.

He started me out in his small five-man company at a "learning wage," when I was thirteen. That's really what a minimum wage is, a learning wage. It's not supposed to support a family. After many years of wage increases I eventually wound up owning the company.

9. www.bls.gov/cps/minwage2012.htm

It's extremely rare for a person who can read, write and speak English to be stuck at the minimum wage for over a year. According to the Bureau of Labor Statistics, 63 percent of minimum-wage workers receive raises within one year of employment.

While it's claimed there's no impact on employment, as government-imposed wage rates rise, so do job qualifications, therefore requiring more experienced workers.

Advocates for increasing the minimum wage apparently believe it's better to have no job than a low-paying one. One result of raising the "learning wage" has been millions of idle, restless teenagers on the streets with a lot of time on their hands for mischief.

Source: Courtesy Mark Perry, prof. of economics, University of Michigan-Flint

The irrefutable evidence from the Department of Labor shows that nearly every time the minimum wage was increased since 1948, unemployment increased. If you track the federal minimum wage, you'll see that unemployment among teens, particularly minorities, increased from 9.4 percent among blacks in 1948 to 32.5 percent in 2004 and from 10.2 percent for whites to 17.2 percent in 2004. Yes, blacks formerly had lower unemployment rates than whites. *(Handbook of Labor Statistics, pp. 153-55.*

To update Nobel Laureate Paul Samuelson's 1976 statement: *"What good does it do a black youth to know that an employer must pay him $9.00 per an hour if the fact that he must be paid that amount is what keeps him from getting a job?"*

There are six official government measures of unemployment; ranging from U-1 to U-6. The media typically reports only U-3. Like the Consumer Price Index (CPI), the definitions of unemployment are changed periodically.

The minimum wage makes many people unemployable while helping a few at the expense of others. Why is this so? Well, economic law tells us that if the price of any good increases people buy less. This is true for gasoline. It is true for cell phones. It's true for blackberries. (I love blackberries. When they are $4.99 a box, I don't buy them. When they're $1.50 I may buy them. When they're 99 cents I buy five boxes at a time.)

It is also true for labor services. Economist Thomas Sowell points out that, *"Every one of us would be 'unemployable' if our pay rates were raised high enough."* You don't think so? Go demand that your boss double your salary right now. Do you think your job would be any more secure if it was the government demanding that your boss double your salary?

When I was young elevators had operators in every car, gas stations had teenagers who washed your windows, pump your gas and checked your oil. Teenagers (including myself) delivered the newspapers and mowed neighbor's lawns.

Continuous increases in the "learning wage" abolished millions of these jobs for teenagers. Petty thefts, vandalism and graffiti by restless teenagers have increased as their job opportunities have decreased.

If increasing wages by edict truly has no significant adverse impacts, as many advocates claim, then we should tell the Chinese, Indian, African and Mexican governments that all that's needed to be as rich as America is to pass a law and simply mandate higher wages.

Notes

Chapter 8

Chapter 9

The 47 percent Who Don't Pay Taxes

"There has never been anything more difficult for man to bear than personal freedom! They say: 'Enslave, but feed us!'"-Fyodor Dostoevsky

Republicans in Congress are so stupid. President Barack Obama set the trap; they walked in. They think Obama's demand to tax the "rich" was about increasing government revenues, even though he said it was not. It's about "fairness."

The Republicans nearly always cave in on budget deficits since government spending has "shrunk" only four times in 62 years: 1954, 1955, 1965 and 2010 when the Tea Party ascended. (These are not the same as balanced budget years).[10]

What are the chances the Republicans will lose the fight over any future "Budget Crisis?" Historically - based on the last 62 years - 16 to one. Budget deficits will never change until more Republicans commit to serving one term for any and all political offices. They have to vote for the good of the country and let the chips fall where they may without endlessly planning for their next election.

The Democratic Party has been the "party of the rich" for decades, led by rich media manipulators. The rich don't mind increases in tax rates so long as the politicians keep giving them tax loopholes.

Seven of the 10 richest members of Congress are Democrats; the three richest Republicans are Michael McCaul, Darrell Issa and Jim Renacci. The wealthiest presidents to occupy the White House have been John F. Kennedy (Democrat), Lyndon Johnson (Democrat), Herbert Hoover (Republican) and Franklin Roosevelt (Democrat).

In "blue" states with a majority of Democrats, the average income is $100,000, while in "red" states with a majority of Republicans; the average income is $30,000, according to Department of Labor Statistics.

10. *www.whitehouse.gov/sites/default/.../fy2013/assets/hist.pdf* *Pg. 21-23.*

Of the 10 wealthiest ZIP codes with political preference, six are represented by Democrats and four by Republicans. As Casey Stengel said, "You can look it up." However, Obama using political jujitsu has brilliantly saddled Republicans with the pejorative "party of the rich."

This is far more important to the President than raising government revenues. It has proven to be a reliable strategy for increasing spending, growing government and redistributing wealth, with the Republicans periodically figuring out how to pay for more government.

The gist of GOP presidential candidate Mitt Romney's comments about 47 percent of the population not paying income taxes was lost in the political game of "Gotcha." Whether the 47 percent is comprised of military, Social Security or welfare recipients misses the point. Assume all 47 percent of the adult population is not legally, ethically or morally bound to pay any income taxes. Assume they all are acting legitimately.

Ask yourself, will half of any country's population for long continue to support the other half (plus paying the government's enormous shipping and handling charges for transferring the payments)?

Consider just Social Security. When monthly benefits started, there were 8.3 million recipients projected for 1940 with a life expectancy of 65 versus a projected 72 million retirees by 2030.

This year, 10,000 baby boomers are retiring each day with a life expectancy of 85 years. These new retirees can expect to receive Social Security payments for an average 20 years while consuming services and products made by others and not reciprocating or contributing any products or services for others (obviously, there are exceptions).

Not all their years of paying into Social Security, even with interest earned, will pay for their extended longevity. For those working, an ever-increasing part of their income will go to people not working.

Through the compromises of Republicans and Democrats, Social Security, Medicare and federal employee future retirement benefits now exceed $86.8 trillion, according to The Wall Street Journal.

To put it in perspective, as Dr. Ben Carson does, count one number per second and it will take you over 2,000 years to count to 86 trillion. Now maybe you can appreciate the magnitude of the problem faced by our children and grandchildren.

"THOSE WHO GIVE UP THEIR LIBERTY FOR MORE SECURITY NEITHER DESERVE LIBERTY NOR SECURITY." --Ben Franklin

The Employee Benefit Research Institute reports that 60 percent of American workers have saved less than $25,000 for retirement, about half a year's median income, not counting Social Security. The $64,000 question is why so many of the 47 percent of the population paying so little taxes look to the government for support?

Perhaps the answer lays in Fyodor Dostoevsky's, *The Brothers Karamazov,* written in 1880. Concerning dependence and freedom compare his description of the government of the Roman Catholic Church with our government today.

The Cardinal of Seville scolds Jesus Christ: "You wanted to come into the world and You came empty-handed, with nothing but some vague promise of freedom, which, in their simple-mindedness and innate irresponsibility, men cannot even conceive and which they fear and dread, for there has never been anything more difficult for man and for human society to bear than personal freedom! For where there is freedom of choice men [can be] bribed with bread? They say: 'Enslave, but feed us!' I tell You once more that man has no more pressing, agonizing need than the need to find someone to whom he can hand over as quickly as possible the gift of freedom with which the poor wretch comes into the world. [By turning stones into] bread you were offered something that could have brought You indisputable loyalty: You would give man bread and man would bow down to You. Man shall not live by bread alone was Thine answer."

---*The Brothers Karamazov* (Bantam Classics, Pg 304-306)

Notes

Chapter 9

Chapter 10

The Gap between Ignorance, Misinformation, Disinformation

"If you don't read the newspaper, you're uninformed. If you read the newspaper, you're mis-informed."   --- Mark Twain

Admiral Hyman Rickover, speaking to the San Diego Rotary on Feb. 10, 1977, stressed, *"A cause of many of our mistakes and problems is ignorance — an overwhelming national ignorance of the facts about the rest of the world."*

Ignorance about the widening gap between the rich and poor is strewn about by the media. "The rich get richer, and poor get poorer." Interestingly Walter Williams, distinguished professor at George Mason University, wrote a column documenting that *"The U.S. has the richest poor people in the world."*

Dinesh D'Souza speaks of a friend in India dying to move to the U.S. Why? *"I want to move to a country where the poor people are fat."*

Informed people realize the only way the majority of poor people in the world get richer is for the already rich to get richer. Rich people create jobs directly or indirectly by investments. Think of Henry Ford, Thomas Edison, the Wright brothers, Bill Gates, Meg Whitman, Steve Jobs, and Warren Buffett. More rich — More jobs — Fewer poor people.

If you don't think rich people create jobs, if you ever become unemploy-ed try asking a homeless person for a job. If you need proof poor people around the world are getting richer, just look at world population.

It took until 1800 for world population to reach 1 billion people, as wars of conquest, confiscation of crops and animals together with slavery, starvation, and early death prevented advancement.

In a little more than 200 years since the Industrial Revolution and the advent of Capitalism (another word for savings), poverty has so diminished that world population this year will reach 7 billion — an impossible feat if the world's poor were not getting richer.

65

Since 1800, per capita income has skyrocketed 10-fold, freeing billions from dependency on their rulers or their governments.

It should be obvious that governments have never created wealth. They consume wealth, through taxation and redistributionist policies, in essence, governments destroy wealth. All government spending is consumption.

Capitalism inherited poverty, began overcoming it and must still fight poverty every day because wealth must be created every day just as food must be created every day.

Countries get rich through production, never simply by consumption of goods, as pointed out by John Stuart Mill.

Marxists at first complained that Capitalism kept the poor both hungry and poor. Now they say Capitalism makes poor people fat.

The census reports that about 15 percent of the U.S. population lives in poverty. It's fascinating to discover in households defined as poor by the government, 80 percent live in an apartment or home with air conditioning.

Nearly 75 percent own a car, and nearly one-third own two or more. The average poor household has two color TVs, a DVD player, microwave, refrigerator, oven, stove, a washing machine and a cordless phone, making them the richest poor in the world.

Using government statistics, the Heritage Foundation reports, *"The home of the average poor family is in good repair and not overcrowded. In fact, the typical poor American had more living space than the average European."* (Average not poor European.)

This is not to say there aren't poor people struggling, but only to acknowledge that things are not as dire as we are misinformed to believe. Both rich and poor in reality are becoming richer.

In fact, the United States' poor today are richer than all but the world's wealthiest people 100 years ago. Politicians keep expanding entitlement programs to capture more of the middle class by calling them poor (their so-called War on Poverty) to garner greater support for the programs and to generate more votes and campaign contributions. Programs that are easy to expand but politically difficult to contract.

My mother, based on her income, was categorized as poor by the government shortly before she passed away. This was because she lived almost entirely on her Social Security, even though she owned a free and clear $600,000 home, free and clear Buick, two TVs, three radios, air-conditioning, a solar panel system, a Spa, and a stock portfolio.

Those who exploit the poor fail to acknowledge that most people start out with low-paying jobs and over time their income increases as they become more competent in a field, more experienced and more productive moving into their peak earning years.

In May 2011, The Federal Reserve Bank of St. Louis published Income Mobility, wherein it stipulated that the wealthiest 20 percent and poorest 20 percent of income households are implicitly and "wrongly" assumed to be the same households over time. "Households" and "Families" are not the same thing in government parlance. Households can be comprised of "one" person or "six."

Over a 10-year period, 58 percent in the lowest quintile moved to a higher quintile. Fifty percent of those in the top quintile fell out of that class, including 57 percent of the wealthiest one percent. Over time there's a lot of movement up and down the income ladder. [11]

Additional misinformation ignores the fact that the top 20 percent of households have more members working (twice as many) as the bottom 20 percent and sometimes the bottom 20 percent of households may have no one employed.

Can you believe it. Some people in government seem surprised that people not working earn less money than people who are working. This is reported as unfair when the numbers are not disclosed.

11. http://research.stlouisfed.org/publications/net/20110501/cover.pdf

Many comparisons between rich and poor do not include transfer payments to low-income households, intentionally misleading.

Imagine not including welfare benefits, food stamps and housing vouchers in calculating the income of poor people.

"There are three kinds of lies: lies, damned lies and statistics," Mark Twain said. Additionally, with today's ubiquitous Internet, there's a lot of "misinformation," often unintentional, as well as intentional "disinformation" hawking the "cost-free compassion" of liberals.

Government is comprised of our neighbors, people like you and me — some smart, some not. Most are not bad people; they're not uneducated, unintelligent or irrational in ordinary matters. Most want to do good.

Until the 1960s it was felt that government employees were selfless, objective advocates of the public good in contrast to people in the private sector concerned only with maximizing their own interests. Dr. James Buchanan won the Noble Prize for "Public Choice" economics modeling that people, whether in government or private enterprise, will promote their own self-interest. This helps explain why the nature of government is to expand and liberty to contract.

It is always a source of amazement why so many people think their neighbors who work for the government are suddenly and eminently qualified to make significant decisions for them. Decisions that affect them and their families, from toilets to tap, to fluoridated drinking water, that go beyond any legitimate public health and safety concerns.

There is no comparison with the knowledge of government employees and that of more than 300 million people in the U.S. who make trillions of decisions a year in what's called "the free market."

The wisdom in the free market (using everyone's knowledge) is a trillion times greater than that of any discrete group of government employees (neighbors), politicians or elites.

In the name of the poor, a lot of people go to Washington to "do good" and wind up doing extremely well for themselves.

Notes

Chapter 10

_____

_____

_____

_____

_____

_____

_____

_____

_____

_____

_____

_____

_____

_____

_____

_____

_____

_____

_____

_____

_____

_____

_____

_____

_____

_____

_____

_____

Chapter 11

"What are taxes for?" ---The Wall Street Journal

When I was on the City Council in the early 1980s a La Jolla doctor testified that taxes were for funding his son's "free" sailing lessons. Otherwise he could not learn to sail. (I'm not making this up). The city at the time owned a flotilla of small sailboats on Mission Bay.

Aircraft owners, after Prop 13 passed, testified that the purpose of taxes was to subsidize city airports and the tie-down fees for parking their planes. Golfers, quite belligerently testified they paid taxes so Torrey Pines golf fees would remain 90 percent lower than comparable world-class courses.

The Chamber of Commerce wanted other people's taxes to subsidize its new motion picture bureau, downtown redevelopment and a new convention center benefiting its downtown members. It successfully convinced the City Council that new convention center hotels should be subsidized by the Transient Occupancy Taxes paid by all hotels and motels not located downtown.

Patrons of the opera, symphony and ballet are absolutely certain the purpose of taxes is to sustain the arts (so $18 of every ticket price at the time was paid for by someone else).

Chargers and Padres fans said heck, if you're gonna subsidize the arts we want our share of the fishes and the loaves -- with billionaire owners and millionaire players egging them on. Talk about "Welfare Kings!" Oh, and to spread the wealth, 54 cents each of millions of admission tickets in the 1980s was paid by the city.

Trolley supporters (who wanted people off "their" freeways) thought the thrill of viewing empty new red trolley cars is why people pay taxes.

Most adamant of all were the Friends of the Library who "demanded" taxes be used to provide free books, videos, magazines and movies. Imagine the money they could raise if the 600,000 "Friends of the

Library" paid a nominal $10 yearly for the 10 million books and video games available to them. Heresy!

People who build, manage, promote or occupy public housing have no doubt the purpose of taxes is to provide "brand new" housing at three times the cost of private apartments so households lacking education or work experience can live splendidly beyond their means. Real estate brokers say no way -- the real purpose is to subsidize FHA and VA loans so they can more easily sell homes.

Attorneys, of course, believe the purpose of taxes is to provide free courts so they can make gobs of money.

Those in the defense industry maintain a higher and perhaps near only constitutional purpose of taxation in this list is to provide for the "common defense" even if it means paying $737 million for every stealth B-2 Bomber (Incredibly, with parts made in 48 states). Indefensible!

We must not forget the whole social services/poverty industry. Social workers "feel" the true purpose of taxes is to pay them to evaluate, investigate, study, manipulate and inform welfare recipients of their unmet entitlements. This is confirmed by some studies showing over 60 percent of money intended for those needing help goes to administration.

From time to time the California Department of Social Services is caught advertising its services in cities in Mexico.

School teachers, at least in California, appear to believe nearly 100 percent of all taxes should go to pay their salaries and pensions, cleverly stating "it's for the children" and lack of higher pay is why so many kids cannot read or write.

However, this is more representative of the Teacher Unions than the majority of truly great and dedicated teachers.

Our university students apparently are taught the real purpose of taxes (along with those rioting in England recently) is to provide practically a free higher education with only token tuitions.

71

Self proclaimed "Saviors of the Earth" believe the purpose of taxes is to save every creature that walks, crawls or flies even if costing millions of dollar each for "Least Bell Vireos," and "CheckerSpot butterflies" that might be saved in Highway right-of-ways. No Darwinian survival of the fittest for so-called "Environmentalists"!

Most recently large numbers of people have maintained the purpose of taxes is to have other people pay their medical and prescription drug bills. Universal "free" health care they call it.

The IRS reported 47 percent of those filing 2009 tax returns paid no "income taxes" and still some argue the purposes of taxes is to pay these nearly 26 million nonpayers over $57 billion annually in "Earned Income Tax Credit" refunds (which weren't "earned" at all).

Presumably the nonpayers of taxes are those who when polled favor increased taxes for other people. Treasury Secretary Timothy Geithner, Congressman Charles Rangel, Senators Tom Daschle and Al Franken make it appear high ranking Democrats favor higher taxes because they have no intention of paying them (until caught).

Then we have a new group of billionaires who say don't look at us, we favor raising income taxes. Distinguished economist Tom Sowell points out however, that income and wealth are not the same thing *"and [the super-rich] still would be billionaires if taxes took 100 percent of their current income."*

Government employees like to echo Justice Oliver Wendell Holmes, *"Taxes are what we pay for civilized society."* (Spoken in 1904 when taxes amounted to 7.6% of income – now closer to 40%).

Our seventh Vice President, John Calhoun, pointed out however, that government employees pay no taxes. There are two great classes he wrote: net payers of taxes and net recipients. If government employees are paid from tax collections it is the taxpayers in reality who pay both the government employees' salaries -- and their taxes -- regardless of what is filed on 1040 tax forms.

Frederic Bastiat noted, *"Government is the great fiction, through which everybody endeavors to live at the expense of everybody else."*

Is it any wonder we're facing a crisis of government? No doubt many reading this believe it's only fair to tax the employers/creators/producers in society and their income and wealth should be redistributed to the takers. The more successful producers become in satisfying consumers, the more their success should be punished by higher taxes.

To them, *"The ideal tax is the one that gets the most feathers out of the goose with the least squawk."*

Income, however, is "earned" not distributed and those demanding re-distribution want it taken from people who earn more money than they do --- never taken from themselves --- for the 95% of the world's population that earns less than them.

It almost makes you want to sit down and cry when you see how by constantly bribing voters, politicians are changing the character of the American people: from one of self-reliance and voluntary exchange to one of "gimee, gimee, gimee," with nearly half the income tax filers now paying no "income tax" at all. (Admittedly, they do pay other taxes).

Notes

Chapter 11

Chapter 12

Kill the Oil Speculators

"It's our land — it's our oil." --- Bill O'Reilly on Fox News

Much of the media and particularly Fox News' Bill O'Reilly have been demonizing speculators for raising the price of gasoline. O'Reilly says the gasoline we buy doesn't belong to the oil companies but to the American people. *"It's our land — it's our oil."*

Karl Marx could not have said it better. It's ours, so let's just take it. Has O'Reilly been taken in by the Occupy Wall Street crowd? Are speculators really evil?

Speculation is universal, even animals do it. Squirrels hoard nuts for the winter, but you never see any newspaper headlines demonizing them. While they are greedy speculators, there's never a front-page exposé about them.

When speculators acquire oil supplies (or even food supplies for that matter), they perform a public service, even if unintentional, as described by Adam Smith's "invisible hand."

Speculators are first to anticipate future shortages when demand will most likely outstrip supply. By acting before events occur, they encourage conservation, and if right and prices rise, they profit. If wrong they lose, sometimes big time.

Speculators also create incentives for greater production. More expensive production techniques become profitable at higher prices and shortages become less severe than would otherwise be the case. When speculators do sell --- prices fall.

Some politicians, if they had their way, would keep prices low, encourage overconsumption, and as a result, we would run out of vital commodities long before they could be resupplied.   They would return us to the days of long gas lines (1973-1974) when some people could only buy on odd days and others on even days.

This was to make it "fair" to everyone, regardless of urgency. Fairness required allocating gasoline by queue rather than price.

In the former Soviet Union, profits were against the law. This often resulted in some essential products not being available at any price.

There was a story about a customer going to the meat counter and ordering a pound (half kilogram) of chicken. The butcher said, *"2-Rubles please."* The customer yelled, *"Are you nuts, chicken is only 1-Ruble across the street."* The butcher said, *"Why don't you go across the street?"* *"Well, they are out today."* The butcher said, *"Well, when we are out, they are only half a Ruble for a half kilo."*

Speculation is everywhere. Farmers, of course, speculate whenever they grow more food than their own families can consume, and which they expect to sell at a profit for more than it costs to grow.

Homebuilders speculate whenever they build more than one home for their own families. Every company that spent $3 million for a Super Bowl ad was speculating they would recover the cost with increased sales and profits.

Even reporters speculate whenever they write a column with the expectation their editor will publish it and keep paying them. All of us are speculators in some fashion.

But the real villains when it comes to speculators always seem to be the oil companies, the favorite boogeyman for many politicians. Politicians want gas prices to come down and home prices to go up. Food prices to come down and farmer incomes to go up. Tuitions to come down and teacher salaries to go up. Go figure! (Yes, it is all about votes).

You would think people who complain about high gas prices would buy oil company stocks to offset higher pump prices. Get their "fair share" of the obscene profits. Exxon Mobil is the most valuable U.S. Company by market capitalization, and Exxon sells for less per share today than it did five years ago. Its profit margin was 9.47% in 2011 (latest figures). So, where are the obscene profits? Many other corporations have higher profits but don't receive the media hostility.

The main culprit for rising gasoline prices, it's apparent, is our own Federal Reserve Bank driving down the value of the dollar. Oil sales worldwide are denominated in dollars, and it is taking ever more dollars to pay for a barrel of oil and hence a gallon of gas.

To make the point you can still buy a gallon of gas today for less than two 1964 "silver" dimes (two selling for $4.14 on 3/22/13).

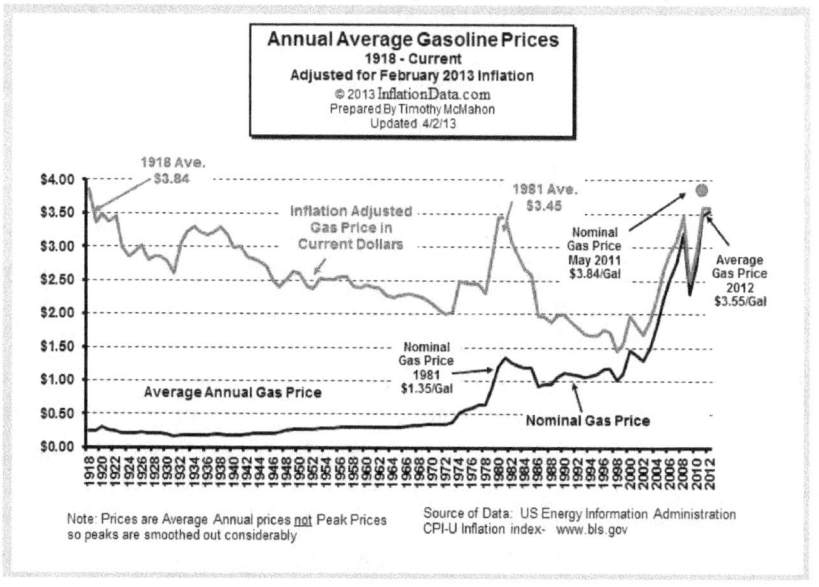

The price of gasoline "adjusted for inflation" as determined by the U.S. Energy Administration, in 1918 was $3.84 per gallon; in 1981, 3.45; and in 2012, it was $3.55 a gallon; or ten cents more than in 1981 and 29 cents less than in 1918.

To summarize. Speculators provide a valuable service when buying into anticipated shortages with the intention of profiting. They bring supply and demand into equilibrium, they induce people to consume less, supplies last longer, nearly always there is some supply without standing in line, plus, they create incentives for new supplies to climb sharply, after which prices drop.

Thank God for speculators.

Notes

Chapter 12

Chapter 13

Oil -- finite but inexhaustible

"The earth will perish in 7 billion years when the sun burns out," my astronomy professor told the UCSD class. *"Repeat that please,"* said a guy nearby, very agitated. After hearing it repeated, with a sigh of relief the student said, *"Phew, for a minute I thought you said 7 million years."*

While we all can agree the sun is finite, the sun's energy is also undeniably inexhaustible. Oil, like the sun, is also finite and inexhaustible. Historically, increases in technology have ensured we need never fear we will run out of oil. Below is a documented series of authoritative predictions dating back to 1885, all warnings the United States will soon run out of oil:

. *1885 - U.S. Geological Survey: "Little or no chance for oil in California."*
. *1891 - U.S. Geological Survey: "Same prophecy for Kansas and Texas."*
. *1914 - U.S. Bureau of Mines: "Total future production limit 5.7 billion barrels, at most 10-year supply remains."*
. *1919 - U.S. Geological Survey: "World oil production will peak in 9 years."*
. *1939 - Dept. of Interior: "Oil reserves in the U.S. to be exhausted in 13 years."*
. *1951 - Dept. of Interior Oil and Gas Division: "Oil reserves in the United States will be exhausted in 13 years."*
. *1952 - Paley Commission report to President Truman predicts oil shortages by 1970s.*
. *1972 - The Limits to Growth report: Group of prominent experts write that 550 billion barrels of oil remained; all known reserves will be entirely consumed by 1992.*
. *1981 - Global 2000 report to President Carter undertaken by U.S federal agencies: Oil will peak by 2000.*
. *2008 - U.S. Department of Defense: By 2012, the surplus oil production capacity could entirely disappear.*

There are two methods for forecasting the cost of anything, the engineer's method and the economist's method. A few years ago, an engineer's method was presented using world "proven reserves" data divided by estimated future consumption and determined that only 37 years of oil remained in the world (not including oil shale).

A question: Would the supply last 37 years at $4.00 per gallon, $1.00 per gallon, or $40.00 per gallon? Predicting peak oil is like trying to count the number of beans in a jar without knowing how big the jar is. How can an engineer tell how much oil remains in the ground without knowing how much there was to start with?

In contrast to the engineer's method is the economist's method. Economists look at the longest possible historical record of resources and ask, are there any reasons to believe resources will become more scarce in the Future?

Furthermore, can you think of any resource that is scarcer today than a hundred, or a thousand years ago? Most strategic resources, the records show, adjusted for inflation, cost less today and therefore are less scarce.

In ancient Egypt only the Pharaohs and the wealthiest people could afford to own copper jewelry. Today, some people will not even stoop to pick up a copper penny.

According to doomsayers, every barrel extracted since oil was first discovered in Titusville, Pa., reduces the finite supply. Despite the fact that every decade since 1859, when oil was first discovered, the known reserves have increased. Obviously, there's a lot more oil being discovered than so-called "experts" want us to believe.

Oil, a miracle of the free market: Just think, oil companies can go halfway around the world, punch a 3-mile deep hole in the ground, suck out the oil, ship it to Long Beach or Louisiana, transport it to a refinery, pipe the refined gasoline to your city, and deliver it to your neighborhood gas station for less money per pound than the U.S. government can mail a first class letter across the street. And Congress wants to prosecute the oil companies, not the post office.

We have been told to brace ourselves for $6 a gallon gas. Soon gasoline will cost as much as bottled water and Pepsi-Cola

There are three revolutionary developments in oil exploration today: super-deep well drilling, oil well replenishment, and Fracking.

Russia and Exxon have drilled 310 wells; deeper than 7 miles, more than twice as deep as most wells and far deeper than any animal and vegetable fossils have ever been discovered. Where there is oil there are no dinosaur bones, and where there are dinosaur bones there's no oil. Could oil come from the earth's mantle, and not fossils? Malthusians and Cornucopians are hotly debating the prospect.

Secondly, 80 miles off the Louisiana coast, Eugene Island Reserve's first well in 1970 started producing about 15,000 barrels of crude oil a day. By 1986 production plummeted to less than 4,000 barrels, soon to be depleted. Suddenly, in 1990, production soared back to 15,000 barrels a day, then 30,000 in 1996. Since then, the amount has been diminishing steadily. There are numerous similar cases.

Oil may be finite, but for all practical purposes, it's inexhaustible. Record high gasoline prices and profits (to pay the $500,000 a day lease for a drilling rig) have resulted in a record number of wells being drilled, which will bring lower gas prices in the future.

Furthermore, there have been recent technical breakthroughs in "Fracking." Pending codes being cracked for various shale deposits, the U.S. is purported to hold more recoverable oil reserves than Saudi Arabia. The California Monterey Shale formation, according to the U.S. Energy Information Administration, is estimated to hold a massive 64% of the recoverable oil from shale (15 billion barrels).

Hydraulic fracturing (Fracking) is similar to the Fluid Catalytic Cracking Unit, which has been used in California for over 50 years. Only it uses a new horizontal drilling technology.

Our biggest obstacle to lower prices is the largest, most powerful cartel in the world --- withholding more known oil reserves than within the entire Middle East --- the United States government.

Notes

Chapter 13

Chapter 14

Why Martin Luther King was a Republican

Barack Obama, when first elected, asked for a dialogue on race. Before beginning at the beginning of institutional racism in the U.S. do you remember Chief Bull Connor in Birmingham, Alabama in the 1960s?

He was the police commissioner who unleashed attack dogs and high-pressure fire hoses on African-American children marching peacefully.

Those TV pictures spread like a Rodney King beating across the country burning indelible impressions on all who watched. Bull Connor changed civil rights forever.[12]

Police Commissioner Bull Connor was a member of the Ku Klux Klan, a racist and even though many people today mistakenly believe he was a Republican, Bull Connor was a Democrat.

Speaking at Vanderbilt University, Condoleezza Rice said that when she was growing up in the South it was Democrats who refused to register her father to vote --- but Republicans did.

Reverend Wayne Perryman, a Seattle minister and the author of *Unfounded Loyalty*, takes us back to the beginning of institutionalized racism in the U.S. In December 2004 he filed a class action suit against the Democratic Party for reparations for its 200 years of oppression. The Democrat Party, from its inception until 1964 was the party of slavery, secession and segregation.[13]

Most people are either a Democrat by design, or a Democrat by deception," writes Perryman. *"They either know the racist history of the Democrat Party and still chose to be a Democrat, or they were deceived into believing it a party that sincerely cared about Black people."*

Rev. Perryman, once a delegate to a Democratic convention is quick to note the Democrat Party of today is not the same as the party of the past.

12. http://www.crmvet.org/images/imgbham.htm_
13. http://www.wayneperryman.com/

Perryman, articulates the following chronology:

1. *"History reveals that every piece of racist legislation that was ever passed and every racist terrorist attack that was ever inflicted on African-Americans was initiated by the members of the Democratic Party, from the formation of the Democratic Party in 1792 to the Civil Rights movement of 1960's. Congressional records show the Democrat Party passed no specific laws to help Blacks and every law that they introduced into Congress was designed to hurt Blacks."*

2. *"History reveals that the Republican Party was formed in 1854 to abolish slavery and challenge other racist legislative acts initiated by the Democratic Party. Some called it the Civil War, others called it the War Between the States, but to the African-Americans at that time, it was the War Between the Democrats and the Republicans over slavery. The Democrats gave their lives to expand it; Republicans gave their lives to ban it."*

3. *"During the Senate debates on the Ku Klux Klan Act of 1871, it was revealed that members of the Democratic Party formed many terrorist organizations like the Ku Klux Klan to murder and intimidate African-Americans voters. The Ku Klux Klan Act was a bill introduced by a Republican Congress to stop Klan Activities. Senate debates revealed that the Klan was the terrorist arm of the Democratic Party."*

4. Perryman's indictment continues: *"From 1792 until 2004, the Democrat Party (America's oldest political party) never elected a Black man to the United States Senate, while the Republicans elected three."*

5. *"During the first civil rights era, it was Abolitionists and Radical Republicans such as Henry L. Morehouse (Morehouse University) and General Oliver Howard (Howard University) who founded many traditional Black colleges. Republicans fought to open them while Democrats fought to close them, which is why several traditional Black colleges are named after white Republicans."*

6. *"In the infamous 1857 Dred Scott decision Court records shows it was the Democrats, with Chief Justice Roger Taney writing the majority opinion classifying Blacks as property rather than people."*

7. *"It was the racist laws of the Democrats that were responsible for two subsequent landmark cases: Plessy v Ferguson (separate but equal) and Brown v. The Board of Education. (Separate educational facilities are inherently unequal)"*

8. *"Congressional records show that Democrats vigorously opposed the 13th, 14th and 15th Amendments (introduced by Republicans) to abolish slavery, give citizenship to all African Americans born in the United States and, give Blacks the right to vote. Democrats voted unanimously against the 15th Amendment."*

9. *"Congressional records prove that Democrats worked hard and long to prevent passage of the following laws that were passed by Republicans to achieve civil rights for African-Americans:*

Civil Rights Act 1866
Ku Klux Klan Act of 1871
Civil Rights Act of 1875
Civil Rights Act of 1957 (Pres. Eisenhower signed, Sen. John Kennedy voted against)"

During the 1960's many Democrats, including Senators Al Gore Sr., Robert Byrd and Sam Erwin fought indefatigably to filibuster the 1964 Civil Rights Act (which passed only because more Republicans voted for it than Democrats).

Democrat Senator Richard Russell addressed the Senate stating, *"We will resist to the bitter end any measure which would have a tendency to bring about social equality and intermingling and amalgamation of the races..."* With 18 Democrat Senators, he organized the longest filibuster (56 days) in Senate history.

After signing the 1972 Equal Employment Opportunity Act and issuing Executive Order 11478, Richard Nixon, a Republican, started what we know as Affirmative Action.

Not widely known, it was three white persons in opposition to the Democrats' racist practices who started the NAACP.

While Democrats would prefer it suppressed, it was Democratic Attorney General, Robert Kennedy who working for his brother the President, who approved secret wire taps and hidden microphones under Dr. Martin Luther King's bed. The tapes were sent to King's wife.

Given the historical record of Republicans and Democrats is it any wonder that Dr. King, like his life-long-Republican father, would be a Republican?

REPUBLICAN MARTIN LUTHER KING KILLED BY DEMOCRAT JAMES EARL RAY

Another thing causing the gnashing of teeth by Democrats is Republican King was murdered by a Democrat, James Earl Ray. Watch the verbal gymnastics Democrats perform in trying to change the public record.

It was Republican President Ronald Reagan who signed the law making Dr. Martin Luther King's birthday a national holiday.

Today, after exclusively giving the Democrats their votes for the past 25 years, Perryman says the average African-American cannot point to one piece of civil rights legislation sponsored solely by the Democratic Party that was specifically designed to eradicate the unique problems that many African-Americans face today. The Congressional record shows that all legislation (since 1964) has had strong bi-partisan support.

So how did the Democratic Party turn things around and get the support of Black Americans? President Lyndon Johnson took a hint from Otto Von Bismarck, father of the modern welfare state who wooed voters by inducing them to become government dependents.

With the right to vote "uppity" African-Americans were becoming the dominant force in Southern politics and so it was imperative that they be co-opted in order to insure the very survival and viability of the Democratic Party.

Johnson was able to contrive the most brilliant public relations turnaround in the history of the United States.

This was done through redistributive economics, by in effect, paying African-Americans to vote for Democrats in spite of the racist history of the Democratic Party.

It was accomplished primarily through promises and concessions and redistribution of trillions of dollars in "entitlement" programs commencing with the "War on Poverty" and the "Great Society" programs. President Obama is right when he speaks of "promises not kept." Promises have been the hallmark of the Democratic Party.

Rev. Perryman admonishes both parties to remember their past. *"The Democrats must remember the terrible things they did to Blacks and apologize and Republicans must remember the terrific things they did for Blacks and re-commit to complete the work that their predecessors started and died for."*

Fred Schnaubelt, a San Diego City Councilman from 1977 – 1981 was San Diego's first elected official to hire an African-American Chief of Staff, Susan Love Brown; he brought Thomas Sowell and Walter Williams to address the City Council and the Urban League; and he was given credit by Clarence Pendleton for his conversion from Democrat to Republican when "Penny," as he was called, was appointed Chairman of the federal Civil Rights Commission.

Notes

Chapter 14

Chapter 15

Ronald Reagan's first political talk a Message to Garcia

"Government is not reason, it is not eloquence — it is force! Like fire, it is a dangerous servant and a fearful master." --- George Washington

Ronald Reagan told me in a one on one meeting just before a major talk that when he first started making political speeches his wife pleaded with him not to make her go to another insufferable political event. He made up his mind that evening, he said, that he was going to entertain first then tell a story to deliver his political message.

Ronald Reagan was called, "The Great Communicator." I told him people don't laugh at my jokes. He said, *"Don't tell jokes, tell stories, humorous stories about the government."* He said in an hour that he was going to tell 500 people a story about the Occupational Safety and Health Administration (OSHA) regulations on how to climb a ladder. Later that evening he told how to firmly grasp the rails and put your left foot on the first step --- to hysterical laughter.

Our times demand political salesmen who can carry a Message to Garcia --- tell the story --- the story to Americans about freedom and why America is an exceptional nation. Who was Garcia? In 1898, at the outset of the Spanish American War, President McKinley needed to get a message to Garcia, leader of the insurgents. An aide said he knew a man, Rowan, who could deliver the message, if anyone could. The president sent for Rowan, handed him the message saying, "Take this to Garcia."

I'm not going to detail how Rowan put the message in a pouch strapped over his back, sailed for Cuba, put in a rowboat off the coast in the dead of night, barely avoided capture, spent 3 weeks in Cuba's jungles to deliver the letter to General Garcia.

The purpose of this classic story is to impress upon you that Lt. Rowan took the letter and didn't ask who was Garcia, where was he, how do I find him, why do you want to send him a letter, or why can't Joe do it. Everyone in this inspirational essay is now dead, but the message lives.

"Civilization is one long, anxious search for just such individuals," wrote Elbert Hubbard. *"Anything such a person asks shall be granted. He or she is wanted in every city, town and village, [every local, state and federal office], the world cries out for such people and they are needed more than ever today -- those who can 'Carry a Message to Garcia.'"*

Politics, probably more than any other profession, demands of a person the extraordinary ability to "Carry a Message to Garcia." Not to romance the voters but inform them, inspire them. I know of no other occupation where the results of a message can change the course of history.

OVER-REGULATED Capitalism

Milton Friedman wrote the typical state of mankind is tyranny, servitude, and misery. Due to the advent of "liberalism" in the 18th century, the Western world is a striking exception. Liberalism originally meant limited government, free markets and private property and still does today in Europe. In America, however, it has come to mean the opposite.

When we speak of freedom, it means freedom from government. Classical liberals, such as Thomas Jefferson, James Madison, and John Stuart Mill understood that more government means less freedom.

Hence, the famous quote, *"That government is best which governs least."* The best government, in other words, is that which fosters an unhampered market economy; variously called Capitalism, the free market or free enterprise.

In 1943 Thomas Watson, Chairman of IBM said, *"I think there is a world market for maybe five computers."* The free market grabbed that idea, ran with it, and is still running. Today we see the results of free enterprise in the computer industry: an exponential increase in computers growing from 5 to over 190 million in just the United States.

Smartphones, an offshoot of computer technology, now number over one billion worldwide. The free market, without significant government intervention, has led to a phenomenal increase in memory chip capacity, simplicity of use, and an enormous increase in productivity for all computer and phone users, and with a simultaneous plummet in prices.

How Facebook was able to surpass a billion dollars while the regulators were sleeping is a fascinating story. It was so new no permission to grow exponentially was needed from Harvard University, the city, the state or federal government, or other states in which it rapidly expanded. Thank goodness for sleeping giants.

Many people today wrongly associate business with free enterprise and expect businessmen to be defenders of the free market. Those people are out of touch with reality.

Professor Ben Rogge in *Can Capitalism Survive?* writes that businessmen, by and large, are not defenders of Capitalism, the profit and loss system, and *"are no more committed to economic freedom than anyone else. Not only are they not the greatest beneficiaries of the system -- they are not even the primary beneficiaries."*

The capable, talented, and strong will survive under any economic system. It is only under Capitalism that the capable, talented and strong get ahead by serving those weaker (consumers) as they wish to be served.

But, as Adam Smith acknowledged, *"[Businessmen] seldom meet together ... but in a conspiracy against the public..."* Most businessmen prefer that government guarantee their profits, underwrite their losses, and limit competition, as done in most other countries whether in computers, oil, shoes, or a thousand other things.

The basic problem of every complex society is how to coordinate the economic activities of large numbers of people.

When decisions number in the trillions every day, it takes the collective wisdom of the free market, the decisions of all the actors, to bring order out of chaos. By contrast, it is impossible for any government to collect all the pertinent data, sort it, correlate it, prioritize it, and act upon it in a timely or efficient manner.

Consider how the free market brings affordable priced food to over 315 million Americans three times a day without any centralized, coercive direction of a government agency, just the voluntary cooperation among farmers, distributors, warehousemen, groceries, restaurants, and consumers all acting in their own "self-interest."

Compare this to the command and control economies of Cuba, and famines of N. Korea, or the former Soviet Union with their paucity of goods with near total government controls and regulations.

"Capitalism," as eminent free market economist Ludwig Von Mises described, *"is that system of social cooperation and division of labor that is based on the private ownership of the means of production. The material factors of production are owned by individual citizens, the capitalists, and the landowners."*

Capitalists, entrepreneurs, and farmers, are instrumental in making free enterprise work and Mises likens them to the helmsmen that steer a ship. None is free however to direct the course, but merely to have their hand on the tiller. They must unconditionally obey the Captain's orders. The Captain is the consumer.

It is the consumers who determine what is to be produced, in what quantity and what quality through voluntary exchanges,. They do this by what they choose to buy or abstain from buying. One year they may want gas guzzling SUVs and the next year compact fuel-efficient cars.

Those who fail to meet the constantly changing wants of the Captain wind up on the rocks and out of business.

"The capitalist system of production," wrote Mises *"is an economic democracy in which every penny gives a right to vote. Consumers are the sovereign people."*

It is the only system that allows for a rational allocation of resources based on what consumers want and are willing to pay for, and not dependent upon the guesswork or favoritism of bureaucrats.

The role of profits in a market economy, when stripped of emotional demagoguery, is to determine what consumers are asking for most urgently. The more urgent the needs, the greater the profits.

Profits are like the gauges on a steam locomotive, which tell the engineer how much steam is required, and how efficient the engine is running. Profits allow for a CEO to sit in the110th floor of the Sears Tower in Chicago and know if his store manager in any city is efficiently running a Sears store.

Profits are the key to the only way in which the general standard of living for all mankind can be raised, and the key is to increase profits, i.e., increase the growth of capital faster than the increase in the population, and improve the methods of production.

Because Capitalism depends on voluntary cooperation and not the coercion employed by all governments throughout history --- it is the only moral economic system ever conceived.

Notes

Chapter 15

Conclusion

If you are not having fun explaining how America became the beacon of freedom and prosperity around the world then perhaps you should choose a difference avocation. If you try to force ideas on people, when they see you coming down the sidewalk they tend to cross over to the opposite side of the street.

Yes, the message is serious and so must be its delivery, but in a smart, friendly package.

It is essential to remember that government is not inherently a necessary evil. *"Government,"* as George Washington purportedly said, *"is not reason, it is not eloquence — it is force! Like fire, it is a dangerous servant and a fearful master."* Government, however, is absolutely indispensable for a free society to work --- but it should act as an umpire in enforcing the rules and should not be playing the game.

Think about it, government is the only organization in society with a legal monopoly on force and violence. It is the only organization that obtains its income not by providing goods and services to others in voluntary exchange, but by force, that is, by the direct threat of confiscation or imprisonment if payment is not forthcoming.

This is why the free market economy (Capitalism) based on voluntary cooperation is the only moral economic system ever devised.

When government interferes in economic affairs, it picks winners and losers, and this engenders hostility by many people towards their government.

When economic decisions are left to the impartial decisions of the free market people are much more apt to accept the results without blaming the government.

Transactions in the free and voluntary market do not occur unless both parties feel, even if sometimes reluctantly, they will be better off after the exchange.

The United States Constitution limited our government more than any government had ever been limited. Our Bill of Rights is a misnomer. It is in reality a series of limits not on the people --- but on the government. Government "shall make no laws" regarding freedoms of religion, speech, press, assembly, etc.

In all places and at all times there have been bullies. The purpose then of government first and foremost is to protect the people from predators, both foreign and domestic, protect property, invoke a common system of justice and enforce contracts legally and voluntarily entered. That's it!

"We have the right people in government," as Milton Friedman was fond of saying, "the trick is to get them to do the right thing." To do this we have to know ourselves what is right, what are the legitimate functions of government, and not ask for so-called "rights" to be paid by others.

A "Right" cannot be a right if it imposes a burden on someone else. That is called enslavement.

Once we know what is the right thing to do --- we can educate our elected officials on doing the right thing. They cannot possibly know on hundreds of issues just because they have been elected to public office. They need our informed and wise counsel. In the Constitution this is known as: "the right to petition the government." (Also known as lobbying).

When government is properly limited, is wedded to a market economy and guarantees private property, you have the three indispensable requirements for a free society.

You and I are the beneficiaries of a land born to freedom, a land of plenty before we were born and that most of us have done nothing to earn. We have an obligation to pass the principles of freedom to our children and to thank God we wake up every morning in America.

About the Author

Hi, I'm Fred,

At my age, I'm thinking ahead and want to go peacefully in my sleep like my grandfather and not screaming like the passengers in his car.

I was born in San Diego and for 50 years (since age 21) struggled to find the best answers to recurring political issues.

So, I'm sharing, while still able, these political nuggets gleaned from researching over 500 books on the most persuasive responses to political issues that never seem to go away.

I would have loved to have a short reference guide like this when I was on the San Diego City Council to respond quickly to these issues when they repeatedly pop up every couple of years; some of which I never heard of before being elected.

I grew up in Casa de Oro (East San Diego County). My family moved and I graduated from Pt. Loma High in 1958. I joined a family cleaning business and in 1968 became a commercial real estate broker. I got ticked off at the government, ran and was elected to the San Diego City Council in 1977 where I served only one term as promised. I have two adult children and have been married 3 times, most recently in 1987 in Moscow, Russia (USSR) to Dr. Irina Antonova.

I need your help in forwarding your comments about the book to your friends or putting them on Facebook in order to reach politicians, Tea Party members and political junkies across the country (and BTW reach my publisher's goal of 10,000 sales). Please note these issues are intended to be the more controversial ones and this Handbook is for providing you with more than "Bumper Sticker" responses to important topics of the day. (Watch for 15 more issues in 2014)

More at http://RomancingTheVoters.com

Notes

Chapter #

ADDENDUM

Humor Supplement for Romancing The Voters People will pay a million times more money to be entertained than educated

15 of the Greatest Political Jokes

Tell some political jokes. I can't they've all been elected

How can you tell when a politician is lying? When he moves his lips!

"Government is like a baby: An alimentary canal with a big appetite at one end and no sense of responsibility at the other" **–Ronald Reagan**

"The most important thing in politics is honesty ---- Once you learn to fake it you're in" **–Sam Goldwyn**

"For me to go into politics would be like sending a virgin into a house of ill-repute" **–H.L. Mencken**

"Politicians and diapers must be changed often, and for the same reason" **–Mark Twain**

I looked up politics in the dictionary, and it a combination of two words: "Poli," which means many, and "tics," which means "bloodsuckers" **–Jay Leno**

Taxing anything less than 100% of your income to some politicians is a tax loophole.

In Sacramento, they call a tax cut "an illegal gift of public funds" **–Ronald Reagan**

He's like Al Gore --- but without the charisma

A true politician can speak on any topic for 2 hours --- and 4 hours if he knows something about it

All the problems in the country today can be traced to the lax immigration policies of American Indians

It doesn't matter who you vote for --- the government always wins

If they don't do it to their wives --- they do it to the country **–Mel Brooks**

Democrats make better lovers. Ever heard of a good piece of elephant? **–Democratic Underground**

Humor aside: Government's not a "necessary evil," not evil at all, but indispensable for a free society which requires private property, and a free market economy protected by a severely limited government.

Political jokes are an American tradition

John Adams is mentally deranged and a hideous hermaphroditical character. **–Thomas Jefferson,** 1800

Blaine, Blaine, James G. Blaine, The Continental Liar from the State of Maine **– Grover Cleveland** 1848 Election

Ma, Ma, Where's my Pa? Gone to the White House, Ha, Ha, Ha **–James Blaine,** 1884 Election

There is no distinctly native American criminal class except Congress. **–Mark Twain** 1835-1910

I don't make jokes. I just watch the government and report the facts. **–Will Rogers** 1879-1935